WOODTURNING TECHNIQUES

the very best from

WOODTURNING

magazine

WOODTURNING TECHNIQUES

the very best from

WOODTURNING

magazine

THE GUILD OF MASTER CRAFTSMAN PUBLICATIONS

GMC Publications Ltd

This collection first published in 1994 by
Guild of Master Craftsman Publications Ltd,
Castle Place, 166 High Street, Lewes, East Sussex BN7 1XU

© GMC Publications Ltd, 1994

ISBN 0 946819 75 0

Designed by Teresa Dearlove

Printed and bound in Great Britain by
Eyre & Spottiswoode Ltd

Front cover photograph by John Hunnex

Contents

Notes on measurements and prices

Measurements: Cautionary note

Although care has been taken to ensure that the imperial measurements are true and accurate, they are only conversions from metric. Throughout the book instances will be found where a metric measurement has fractionally varying imperial equivalents (or vice versa), usually within ⅟₁₆in either way. This is because in each particular case the closest imperial equivalent has been given, so that a measurement fractionally smaller will be rounded up. For this reason it is recommended, particularly on the smaller projects, that a drawing is made of the work in imperial sizes to ensure that the measurements have not lost anything in the translation. (See also the Metric Conversion Table, page 111.)

Also, although the measurements given here are carefully calculated and are accurate, some variation may occur when pieces are hand turned, so care must be taken and adjustment may be necessary as the work progresses.

Prices

Prices shown in the articles in this volume were correct when originally published in *Woodturning* magazine. Readers should check current prices with the suppliers before ordering items mentioned.

Introduction

When I took over the editorship of *Woodturning* magazine in early 1992, I was aware that I was inheriting from founder–editor Bernard Cooper a little gem of a publication.

From the very first issue, each magazine has contained a wealth of ideas, information and inspiration specifically designed for woodturners – something that had been clearly lacking prior to the launch of the magazine at the end of 1990.

Here was a gold mine of talented authors, some with worldwide reputations as established experts and professional artists, others unknown amateurs who could nevertheless proudly claim the title of expert in their chosen field.

Some may have thought the seam of gold would soon be worked out. I am delighted to say that the seam has not only continued but has grown in both quality and quantity from those early days. With each new issue of *Woodturning* comes not the question, 'What shall we put in', but rather, 'What on earth do we leave out?'

Of course, different articles appeal to different readers. Raw beginners are keen to find advice and tips on basic techniques. Others are looking for projects they can try in their own workshops. Yet more are looking for features on the most innovative artists and their work as a source of fresh inspiration.

But our technical articles, usually concentrating on particular techniques, or the 'how-to' of the craft, have always proved particularly popular.

In this volume we have collected together some of the very best of the technical articles from the first 19 issues of *Woodturning* magazine. This is in part a response to the many readers who write in asking for articles from back issues. So popular has the magazine become that, sadly, many back issues are now out of print and no longer available.

Here you will find ideas for new ways of turning, new tools and materials for turning, different finishing techniques, tips on seasoning, sharpening, adapting tools for machinery – even sandblasting. In face a whole range of ideas to keep woodturning enthusiasts busy for many happy hours.

I hope you will enjoy reading – and trying – these ideas as much as I have enjoyed editing them for *Woodturning*. May this book, and the magazine, continue to provide inspiration for turners for many years to come.

Nick Hough
Editor, *Woodturning*

Turning Tagua

It was like a breath of fresh air when I first learnt about Tagua nuts, or vegetable ivory.

Ernie Conover

One of my pet peeves is that most turning discussions seem to prattle on endlessly about bowl turning to the exclusion of anything else. Get a group of turners together and it is just bowls, bowls, bowls. Come on folks, there are other things that can be turned on the lathe. In fact my friend Leo Doyle, who shares my annoyance at bowl mania, even has a list of several hundred non-bowl items that can be made on the lathe. He hands it out to his students at California State University, San Bernardino, where he teaches a wood programme.

So it was like a breath of fresh air when I first learned about Tagua nuts, or vegetable ivory. The air has been bittersweet, however, because most turners simply turn miniature cremation urn-like vessels from the versatile ivory nut. They totally overlook the plethora of interesting turning projects that the nut offers. Throughout my turning career it seems I have gained more from the past than from the present. Much of what is being discovered today is simply rediscovery of lost art from former times. So it is that I have looked to what the Victorian turners did with Tagua and found much.

The Tagua nut is the seed of two subspecies – *Phytelephas macrocarpa, Palmae* or *Phytelephas aequatoialis, Palmae*. These are commonly referred to as ivory palms. The palm occurs in groves along wet river-bottom lands in South America. Although ivory palms grow in Southern Panama, Columbia, Ecuador and Peru the best nuts have traditionally come from trees growing along the Madgalenea River in Colombia. (And you thought only cocaine came from Colombia?) The palm lives from 50 to 100 years and produces seed after five to eight years.

Most of the ivory species grow erect, however, there are subspecies the trunks of which grow along the ground. A mature tree reaches 6 – 12 metres (20 – 40ft) and the profile looks much like the familiar coconut palm. On a mature tree, small white fragrant flowers occur at the base of the leaves. Over time these

mature into a rough seed pod or burr. It looks much like the burr around the common American horse chestnut. (This is the Ohio state tree, often called a buckeye, hence Ohioans are called Buckeyes.) A single burr contains from 30 to 90 Tagua nuts and weighs 20 to 25 pounds. A single tree produces from six to eight burrs per year so some simple math tells us the average output is about 350 nuts per year. Nuts vary from the size of walnuts to large hen eggs. It takes a full year from flower to fully ripened fruit. At this point the burr splits at the bottom and the nuts fall to the ground. They have an outer shell which is covered with an oily substance. The ripened nuts are quite eatable and are often gnawed by animals. In fact, the Indians extract a liquid from the nuts as a refreshing drink. My two Labradors seem to love the dried nuts and will happily chew on one for the odd half hour with little damage to the nut other than some scratch marks.

Birth of the button trade

As the seed dries out it gradually becomes hard, forming a natural plastic-like substance that closely resembles ivory. About 130 years ago the ivory nuts made their way to Hamburg, Germany. From Hamburg they made their way to Hamspach, Austria, a town noted for carving. The carvers sawed the nuts into slices and carved them into buttons which were a big hit at a fair in Vienna. And so, the ivory nut button trade was born.

Tagua nuts made their way to England a bit earlier than in the rest of Europe. Exact dating is difficult, but it was a gradual thing in the 1820s and 30s. At that time they were often called Corrozzo nuts. (There were many spellings, Corozo being a common one. Holtzapffel's volumes use both Corosos and Coquilla.) This name was that used for the nut by the Taguaros gatherers, who were black people brought in to the area as part of the slave trade and after whom the Tagua nut is now known.

Although Victorian English turners made a variety of interesting objects from Corozo, it was for buttons that the substance was found most suitable. Around the time of the American Civil War, ivory nut button factories were established in France, England and Leeds, Massachusetts. By the 1880s there were also factories in Canada and Rochester, New York. It is recorded that in 1887 the factories at London and Birmingham, England, used two to three million nuts a year.

Victorian need for ivory nuts became so intense that ivory palm plantations were established in South America to simplify gathering. Ivory nut was a real cash crop! In this century plastics like celluloid and bakelite gradually replaced vegetable ivory and the jungles were allowed to take over again. Today, however, the

content of this precious resource rather than letting it go up in smoke. One of the best suggestions is that if you, as a woodworker, want to do something about this problem, levy yourself a tax of 25 per cent of the purchase price of any tropical species you use. Donate this money to one of several conservancies trying to buy tracts of rain forest. While these tracts may not change global climate trends which the destruction may be causing, they will provide gene pools to help our children correct our follies.

One such organisation is Conservation International based at 1015 18th Street, Suite 1000, Washington, DC, USA, telephone 202-429-5660. They recently launched The Tagua Initiative, 'a

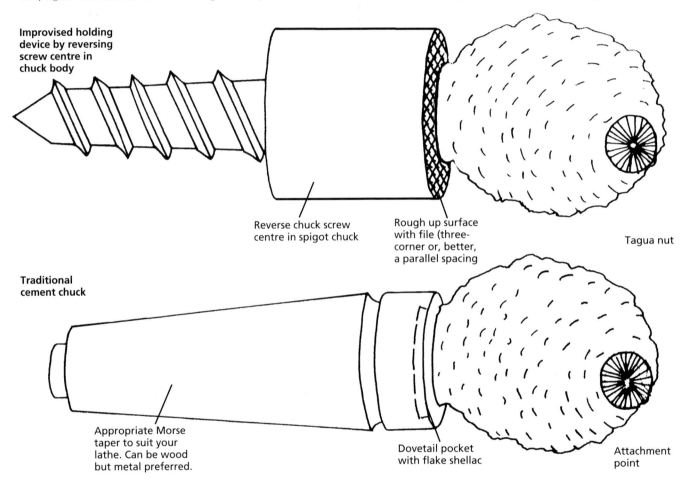

Improvised holding device by reversing screw centre in chuck body

Reverse chuck screw centre in spigot chuck

Rough up surface with file (three-corner or, better, a parallel spacing

Tagua nut

Traditional cement chuck

Appropriate Morse taper to suit your lathe. Can be wood but metal preferred.

Dovetail pocket with flake shellac

Attachment point

pendulum may have swung in the opposite direction. There is growing world concern over the present wholesale destruction of tropical rain forests. As woodturners we are painfully aware of the growing controversy over the morals of using tropical timbers.

Rain forests

Current thinking in the United States is that the vast, vast majority of the destruction of tropical rain forests is due to short-sighted governmental economic policies which encourage 'slash and burn' agriculture. Woodworkers in general, and woodturners in particular, use only an infinitesimal part of the rapidly shrinking pool of tropical species. The fact is that we at least fix the carbon

flagship programme designed to bolster markets for ecologically sound forest products for the benefit of local communities'. In a licensing agreement with two major US sportswear clothing companies – Patagonia Inc. and Smith & Hawken – the Tagua button industry may be reborn. These two companies, with much ballyhoo, agreed to put 'ecologically sound' Tagua buttons on all of their clothing starting in 1991. Under the agreement, Patagonia and Smith & Hawken will together purchase one million buttons made from Tagua as well as pay a licensing fee to Conservation International.

In fairness to Patagonia and Smith & Hawken, their participation in the programme is altruistic, benevolent and charitable. At the right level of production The Tagua Initiative will be a wonderful programme which should bring cash to an impoverished area. Conservation International is encouraging the locals to revere the ivory palm for its cash crop value and not to cut it down. Further, they are encouraging plantings in areas that have been cleared for cattle raising – Tagua plantations. The cycle has gone full circle. If all this fails, Conservation International is heavily into acquiring land, to provide the gene pool of tropical species for our children to correct our mistakes.

Ornamental turners

The Tagua nut was also a common material for ornamental turners. Antique shops abound with thimbles, tape measures and needle cases made from Tagua on ornamental lathes.

Collectors of such items easily distinguish Tagua from elephant ivory or whalebone. Tagua has a definite pattern, much like a thumb-print, which can be seen on any polished surface. The best place to look is on any bead. A little practice and a hand lens will make a Sherlock Holmes of anyone at positive identification of Tagua.

The Victorians got around the problem of the nut's size by simply cutting threads and screwing two and three nuts together. Fairly common are needle cases made in three pieces – a body with a cap at either end. One of my favourite things to make out of Tagua is thimbles. It makes good use of the material and is something useful, unlike miniature cremation urns.

Turning Tagua

To turn Tagua one has to understand the nut's structure. Nineteenth-century factories had to dry the nuts, as they were shipped from South America as harvested. Today's agricultural laws will not allow this, as pests can travel with the cargo. Therefore, the nuts are dried and fumigated at the source before export. Depending on the exporter, a nut may or may not have an outer shell which is smooth and the colour of mud. In any case, it is easily removed by a sharp rap on the bench top. The nut itself has a rough brackish-brown surface looking much like tree bark.

Careful inspection will reveal where the nut was attached while in the burr. From this point a fissure radiates to the centre of the nut. This is a space reserved by nature to allow for the germination of a new ivory palm. It is an affliction to the turner because its size is unpredictable! Band sawing a few nuts from the attachment point through the middle will quickly give you the idea. I have turned nuts ranging from no perceptible fissure at all, to caverns that rendered them useless. Rather than cause consternation, I just look at it as part of the fun.

These parts are also perfect for one of my favourite uses of Tagua – inlays. I like to inlay the end of turned handles and lids with a bit of ivory nut. I simply cement chuck the piece and turn a disc. I then scrape a pocket in the item I want to inlay and glue the Tagua into place. If you turn a bit of taper to the disc and scrape the pocket carefully, glue is almost not needed. I prefer hide glue but almost any glue will work. To correct a bad fit, cyanoacrylate (superglue) or epoxy glue is probably best. As the saying goes,

'Without putty, paint and glue what would the *poor* carpenter do?'

If you are turning anything vessel-like, be it a cremation urn or a thimble, the fissure just saves you excavation time. If you are turning knobs or finials, there are several approaches. One is to section the nut and turn from the parts. A second is to glue several of the pieces together. With careful disc sanding and modern glues the results are excellent. The third is to drill a 1.5mm (¹⁄₁₆in) hole into the fissure at the attachment point. Fill the fissure with water-thin cyanoacrylate glue and allow it to dry in a warm place for a day or two. The result is a solid nut that works well. If you do hit the fissure it only leaves a clear spot that looks quite natural.

Chucking is not hard at all. Most turners use the trusty cyanoacrylate glue, but in a medium viscosity. Use of an accelerator will cause this adhesive to set in 30 seconds to one minute. However, most accelerators contain Freon TA, which is the stuff that is eating up the ozone. Mount a piece of sound timber plank grain on a faceplate and turn a bit of a pedestal for the nut. Sand a small flat spot on the Tagua and glue it on the pedestal. Using a centre in the tailstock can help to get the nut glued in the best position to produce the greatest yield.

Cement chuck

Being a traditionalist, I prefer what watchmakers call a cement chuck. My adaptation of this classic chuck is a Morse taper blank with a slight depression turned in the end. The taper can then be heated with an alcohol lamp and flake shellac melted into the depression. Sand a flat spot on the nut and place it firmly in the hot shellac. Once cool, you have a secure hold. If you do not like the positioning, heat the centre/shellac and move the nut. Easy, reversible and the ozone is safe. An alcohol lamp is best for this as it is not too hot. Be careful not to overheat; the trick is to just melt the shellac but not to boil it. If it bubbles the shellac will be weakened and will not hold well. This chuck can be improvised. I have even used the end of a wood dowel in a pinch – it was singed a bit, to be sure, but it worked. For those with one of the several collett chucks, reversing the screw centre or chucking a steel bar will work quite nicely.

Turning is straightforward. I usually start with spindle gouges ground to a long fingernail. I then move to scrapers and finally remove the toolrest and hand hold a cabinet scraper. Sanding starts with 180 grit and proceeds to 520/600. I then take a small felt wheel on a stub arbor, which can be chucked in an electric drill, and buff the surface with grey steel compound. I do this while the piece is revolving in the lathe. The result is a mirror finish which shows the characteristic Tagua pattern in the material. I have tried jewellers' rouge but find it stains the work noticeably. Grey steel compound is just the ticket.

It is possible to turn hollow Tagua turnings to very thin and uniform walls. While this may seem amazing to the casual observer, it is not, and in fact is just a parlour trick. Shine a bright light at about 3 o'clock on the work and you will be able to see the tool inside the turning as it becomes thin. You will be able to judge very accurately the thickness of the wall by the translucence. Also, a soda straw is invaluable for removing debris from a small

Turning a thimble

1. Cement chuck
The attachment point or fissure on the nut is towards the tailstock and will be removed when turning commences.

Attachment point – i.e. where the nut was attached to the burr!

2. Turn outside of thimble then hollow out inside. If user available, you can custom-fit. Cut off just ahead of chuck face.

3. Turn dowel in chuck or faceplate to *exact* inside shape of thimble. Tap thimble on to taper and finish end. If thimble slips on taper, use a little rubber cement. Use of indexing, in combination with a Dremel tool and the tool rest, allows for decoration of end. This decoration is useful, as it traps the needle and prevents slipping.

Glue dowel in disc on faceplate

Original nut

4. Finished thimble
Looks just like ivory – and the elephants are safe!

Decorate end with Dremel tool and small burr or corebox bit. Use indexing and guide Dremel with tool rest.

opening. Simply insert the straw into the interior and blow out the rubble.

A hex wrench (known as an Allen wrench in the US and an Allen key in the UK) makes an excellent improvised scraper for internal turning through small openings. Simply epoxy the wrench in a small handle and grind the end of the right-angle bend to a scraper of the desired shape. You may have to shorten the length of the right-angle bend depending on the need. A hex wrench is slightly hardened (about 45° Rockwell C) so makes a dandy scraper. Be sure to turn a handle of robust diameter so that you can have relaxed but firm hold, for it is easy for such a tool to spin with the work with catastrophic results. Above all, have fun!

This article originally appeared in *Woodturning* issue 2, Winter 1991.

5. Hex wrench scraper for internal turning

Glue in handle

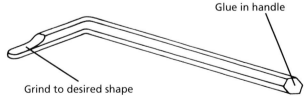

Grind to desired shape

Turning a deep oval bowl

The ancient art of oval turning is poised to enjoy a revival now that novel high-speed turning lathes (OTL) are being developed. Here one of its leading exponents describes the turning of an oval bowl.

Johannes Volmer

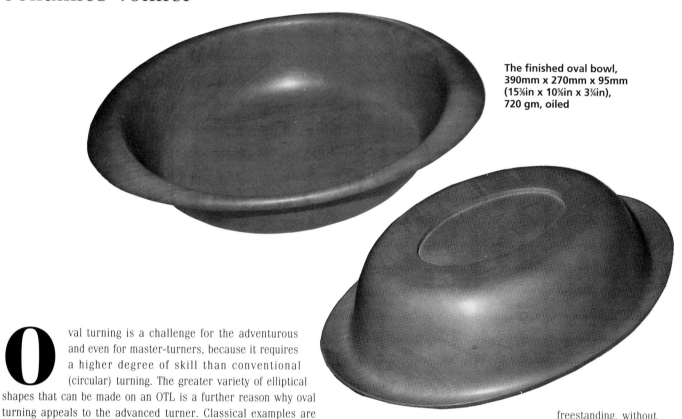

The finished oval bowl, 390mm x 270mm x 95mm (15⅜in x 10⅝in x 3¾in), 720 gm, oiled

Oval turning is a challenge for the adventurous and even for master-turners, because it requires a higher degree of skill than conventional (circular) turning. The greater variety of elliptical shapes that can be made on an OTL is a further reason why oval turning appeals to the advanced turner. Classical examples are oval picture and mirror frames, plates, shallow bowls, keyhole plates and other furniture features and decorations.

For the design of objects with elliptical cross section the creative turner has one dimension more than the turner of round pieces. The ellipse is a curve of traditional charm and elegance. We are surrounded by the ellipses of the planets, and we like to see portraits and our mirror image within elliptical frames.

The early oval turning lathes as described in old books, e.g. *Ornamental Turning* by Holtzapffel, were slow; they disappeared decades ago as production machines (see 'The Oval Lathe – History of Oval Turning' in *American Woodturner* vol.4, no.4 (June, 1990)). With the modern OTL, woodworkers can turn elliptical pieces from hard and soft wood at the same cutting speed that is used for producing cleanly cut surfaces of round pieces on a normal lathe.

The high speed of the new OTL is possible because its moving parts are dynamically balanced just like the wheels of a car. Also the complete balancing is good enough to use the OTL freestanding, without rigid attachment to the floor or working table. Thanks to its construction, the latest OTL mechanism has no slider and needs no lubrication or other maintenance. It runs quietly and without the slam-bang that was characteristic of previous oval lathes.

The new OTL are the result of research, development and testing over many years. They can be built in a variety of sizes to accommodate the turning of elliptical pieces of a wide range of diameters and weights. With the increasing interest in extending traditional turning techniques and applications into fresh fields, it is expected that lathe manufacturers will begin to supply the new high speed OTL in the fairly near future.

So as to explain what oval turning today really means, I will describe the process of turning a deep oval bowl with rolled-over rim. The essential differences between normal (circular) and oval turning techniques will not be mentioned here; they are described in detail already and by sketches in other publications. (See *American Woodturner*, vol.5, no.1 (Sept. 1990) and no.2 (Dec. 1990).)

1. The oval lathe with centreplate and slider, the prepared pear wood blank, an auxiliary hardwood board and scales

2. Screwing the aux-board onto the slider and weighing the blank

3. Chucked blank ready for oval turning

4. Setting a marker in equidistant points of the centreline generates a series of coaxial ellipses

Chucking

A pear wood blank was prepared years ago from a freshly cut log. Its shape was roughly chainsawn and the inside hollowed as usual between pins on my circular lathe for quicker and better seasoning in the open air. The measurements of the blank were 55mm x 300mm x 110mm (19⅝in x 12in x 4¼in). This volume I estimated would be sufficient for a deep elliptical bowl of rural style with a rolled-over rim, profiled like hat brims, at the major sides of the axis for easy handling when the bowl is filled with, for example, bread or fruits. After making a number of different sketches I gained a clear concept of the design of the piece, its profiles and cross sections.

Photo 1 shows the centreplate of my heavy oval lathe with the slider, the tool rest, an auxiliary board and scales for weighing the blank. The scales in Photo 2 show the weight of the blank – 5.3kg.

Instead of a metal chuck, I use an auxiliary hardwood board screwed onto the slider with four M6 (metric 6mm (¼in)) flat head metal screws. Aux-board weighs 1kg; it has been used many times before as can be seen by the numerous screw holes.

The blank must be planed on its upper face to ensure it fits snugly onto the aux-board (Photo 3). It is secured to the board from the rear side by four 8mm (⅜in) hex head wood screws. The screws must be set in areas of the blank that later on can be turned or cut off. Properly locating screws requires carefully taking into account the piece's final shape.

Counterbalance adjustment

The half-axes' difference I intended for the external and internal walls of the bowl is 30mm (1⅛in), i.e. the ring of the oval mechanism must be shifted 30mm (1⅛in) off centre and fastened. This is the first adjustment to be made before turning. The second concerns the counterbalance device. The half-axes' difference and the weight of the blank (5.3kg) and the aux-board (1kg) determine the radius of the countermass. The oval turner gets this radius from a diagram without any calculation. The countermass is easily adjustable by a spindle up to its right radius shown on a dial (not to be seen on the photos).

Turning the bowl's exterior

Turning is started with roughing the face and the exterior side of the blank in small steps, not overcrowding the cut of the gouge, until the elliptical shape has been worked out and the blank trued.

For demonstrating an ellipse series on the face I set a marker in equidistant points on the centreline while the work is running (Photo 4). The centreline is the horizontal line going through the spindle centre and orthogonal to the spindle. It is lightened by a halogen slide projector. The projector generates a light plane that is exactly oriented to the centreplane, i.e. the horizontal plane going through the spindle axis. The cutting line is the curve within the centreplane along which the cutting point or area of the tool's edge must be guided.

Photo 5 shows the resting work with the ellipses on its face and the lightened centreline or cutting line.

The next step (Photo 6) is roughly turning the face, that means the bottom of the bowl, and its external side. Refining the shape by light cuts, with a narrow 12mm gouge, follows. The gouge has an edge with acute fingernail profile and small wedge angle for softwood cutting conditions (Photo 7). At the side of the work the gouge cuts the wood only with a short arc of its edge. This cutting arc must be guided accurately along the intended profile line located in the centreplane.

5. Series of ellipses on the bottom of the bowl. The centreline is illuminated.

6. Turning the outer shape. The cutting edge point is guided along the illuminated (lightened) cutting line.

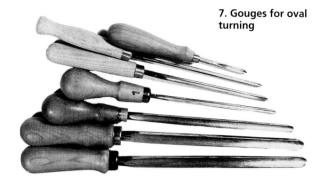

7. Gouges for oval turning

The ellipse series on the bottom of the running work is visible only along and nearby the centreline. The heavy work whirls at about 350 rpm resulting in an average cutting speed of 5 m/s at the external side. This is a minimum speed rate for shear cutting softwood fibres and consequently obtaining clean-cut surfaces. Skilful handling of the gouge is nonetheless necessary. Care is to be taken with finishing the upper area of the exterior bowl wall, and the under side of the rolled-over rim, with a narrow gouge having the edge shape mentioned above.

Next (Photo 8) the rabbet is turned into the bottom of the bowl with a gouge, the flank and the corner of the 6mm (¼in) deep rabbet being cut exactly in the centreplane with the long point of a skew chisel, and the bottom of the rabbet planed with a scraper.

Sanding the bottom and the outside surface is demonstrated in Photo 9. The sandpaper must be pressed against the work only in the centreplane area. The other parts of the gyrating work do not allow a permanent touch of the wobbling surface.

Hollowing the bowl

The next steps are unscrewing the work from the aux-board and screwing on a beechwood board for turning the jam-fit chuck (Photo 10) that exactly fits the oval rabbet in the bottom of the bowl. Both the rabbet and the stub of the jam-fit chuck should be turned slightly tapered to ensure the work is held safely in the chuck.

After roughly bandsawing the outer elliptical contour of the overhanging rim (the parts with the screw holes are cut off). I weighed the work again; its weight was now 2.3kg. For this weight

I had to adjust the countermass on a radius newly received from the diagram.

The work is hammered onto the jam-fit chuck after having carefully ascertained the right position of the rabbet relative to the stub of the jam-fit chuck. A circular rabbet fits in every position onto its stub but not the elliptical recess onto its elliptical stub. Finding the right position requires some feeling. In a wrong position one can easily damage the recess; the work would not be held firmly in the jam-fit chuck. Above all the outer and inner ellipses would not be coaxial, that means the thickness of the bowl's wall would not be constant.

Turning the inside wall and bottom is done from the rim towards the bottom and finally with light cuts, in many steps, along a cutting line exactly located in the centreplane (Photo 11).

In Photo 12 the interior profile of the bowl, in spite of its running and whirling, is clearly to be seen from the lightened cutting line in the centreplane. In Photo 13 the lathe is stopped, the work at standstill.

10. Hardwood board with oval turned tapered stub for jam-fit chucking the oval board

11. Hollowing the bowl with a gouge guided along the lightened cutting line

Having finally turned the interior wall and bottom of the bowl in the desired shape, I began sanding. The sandpaper must be pressed in the area near the centreplane as described above. The grits were chosen as is customary for bowl turning, depending on the smoothness of the turned surface and on the wood and grain.

For shaping the outer elliptical rim contour, I chose an ellipse with greater half-axes difference (Photo 14). For that ellipse the ring of the oval mechanism was set off centre 55mm (2⅛in). I cut the bowl rim with the gouge guided parallel to the lathe spindle but had to pay attention to the fact that the edge of the rolled-over rim is not located in a plane. The reason is the distinction of the ellipses. The gouge does not cut continuously but with interruptions twice per

8. Turning the recess for jam-fit chucking

9. Sanding only in the centreplane area

12. Inside shape finished, bowl runs but cutting line (lightened) at standstill

13. Bowl at standstill, cutting line (profile) lightened

14. Turning the outer shape of the rolled-over rim

15. Rounding the edge of the rim by filing and sanding

revolution. This never occurs with rims of circular bowls. Turning such an exterior elliptical contour requires some care.

Last, I rounded the rolled-over rim's sharp edges with files and sandpaper; for the reasons mentioned above the final profile of the rim cannot be completely finished by turning only (Photo 15).

The finished bowl is removed from the jam-fit chuck by gently knocking with the hand onto the outer wall near the bottom of the bowl. The weight of the finished bowl is 720 grams, and its measurements are 390mm x 270mm x 95mm (15⅜in x 10⅝in x 3¾in). The minimum wall thickness is 6 – 7mm (¼in).

Oval turned object design

All rules for designing objects that can be turned on a lathe are valid and applicable for designing oval turned pieces.

However, there are some exceptions caused by the geometrical properties of the oval lathe and of the work's gyrating motion.

In general, oval pieces must be designed as facework. In principle, oval turning of centrework is possible and offers an immense variety of forms but it requires a specially equipped oval lathe. I intend to write about this technique in another article.

In comparison with circularly turned objects, the designer has at his disposal one additional parameter besides the profile for designing the shape of the elliptical facework object. This parameter is the difference of the ellipses' axes. The designer can choose a certain value of this difference for the entire object or he takes a different value for each part of the object. For instance, I turned the body of the deep oval bowl with 60mm (2⅜in) difference and the rolled-over rim with 110mm (4¼in) difference.

For better explanation, let me compare a turned object with a globe. It has a rotational axis and longitudes (meridians) and latitudes, and we see these lines as circles building the grid on the surface of the globe.

Designing a circularly turned object means finding the form of the longitude as the object's profile. The longitude is a curve that

lies within a plane going through the rotational axis. The latitudes are by all means concentric circles around this axis.

The design of an oval turned object demands two decisions concerning the form of the longitude and the form of the elliptical latitude characterized by the axes' difference mentioned above. Note that the oval turned object has no rotational axis but a central axis located in the centre of the elliptical latitudes. The longitude, the object's profile to be found by the designer, lies within a plane but this plane does not go through the central axis in every position. I would like to explain these relations below by means of an oval turned bowl design.

Richard Raffan's excellent book *Turned-Bowl Design* (The Taunton Press, Newtown/Connecticut,1987) comprises the author's experience and knowledge as a successful longtime bowl maker. He constitutes rules for designing well-shaped bowls, and as far as I understand his texts I guess all his statements and results could be directly transferred to oval-turned bowl design. His chapters on converting timber to bowl blanks, and rough-turning and seasoning the blanks, seem to be applicable without any restrictions to oval bowl making.

Richard Raffan's statements on forms and profiles of bowls are illustrated in his book by many drawings showing the central line, i.e. the bowl's rotational axis, the profile line, that is in general a curve, and the bottom line or the foot of the bowl. Following the terms I proposed above the reader sees in Richard Raffan's drawings the longitude of the bowl.

In order to get an idea of the circular bowl's spatial shape, you have the longitude revolve around the axis. You can easily imagine the consequence of a profile made from arcs, of shallow or deeper out flowing profile lines, of symmetric or asymmetric concave curves or of ogee curves and of those with rolled-over rims.

Richard's suggestions for profiles underline the versatility of bowl design. Looking at one of his proposed bowl profiles I was trying to get full comprehension of the shape and spatial effect of an oval bowl with this profile in it. But it is hard to comprehend how the oval bowl would look in three dimensions. Due to the elliptical latitudes, the oval bowl changes its shape, if you look at the bowl from a certain point of view and if you revolve it around its central axis. This change is entirely contraversal to any circular bowl.

Designers usually sketch the objects they draft by hand, but I notice that even trained designers are not able to draw an elliptical object precisely in perspective views. To me it seems to be impossible to get an exactly drawn view of an oval piece without application of geometrical laws. For this reason I wrote computer programmes for easily and quickly screening and plotting views of bowls I intend to make. Since designers have applied computers for many years, my proposal to use computer graphics also for turned object design – especially for those objects with very complicated shapes like oval bowls – should be found acceptable. The designer can have lots of shapes drawn in a very short time and thus ensure himself, at minimum cost, that his choice will meet the tastes of his customer.

With Figs 1 and 2 I am going to explain briefly the computer-aided design of a simply shaped oval bowl. The input is the height

Fig 1 Main plane drawings of an elliptical bowl with parabolic profile (longtitudes)

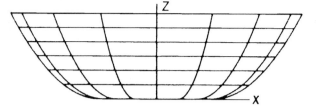

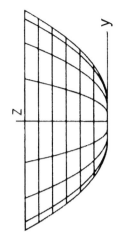

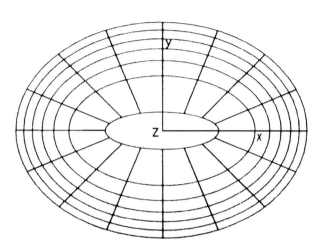

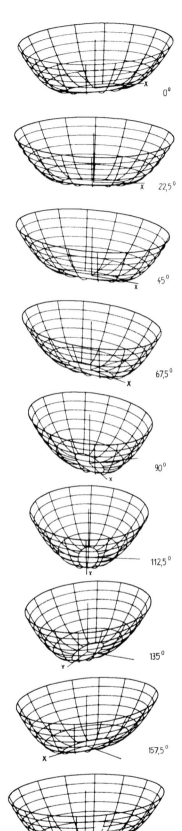

of the bowl, the lengths and difference of the axes of the latitude ellipse of the bottom or the rim and last but not least, the profile. You can input any profile you want, either drafted freely by hand or mathematically described. For instance, parabolas, circles or straight lines.

Fig 1 shows the three main plan drawings of an oval bowl, with parabolic profile as longitude and seven equidistant ellipses as latitudes, including the bottom and the rim ellipse; the wall thickness is neglected. The ground-plan demonstrates that the longitude or its extension does not go through the central axis in any position. That means, an arbitrary central cross-section of an oval bowl does not reveal its real profile. You must cut the bowl along the ellipses' axes only in order to see the profile you have turned.

In Fig 2 the bowl is to be seen from a certain spatial point of view perspectively, in positions received by twisting the bowl around its central axis for half a revolution in steps of 22.5°. There were friends who doubted that the drawings are exact, that the bowl could have these shapes, but it really has. I am sure that oval bowl design could be an interesting subject of debate among advanced turners.

Readers who wish to know more about the oval turning lathe, or rather the oval chuck, should turn to volume 5 of Holtzapffel's monumental work, *Turning and Mechanical Manipulation*, where he describes and illustrates the oval chuck that appeared in Peter Nicholson's *Mechanical Exercises* some 72 years earlier. The chuck used by Professor Volmer resembles the one illustrated in Holtzapffel.

On visiting our office, Professor Volmer readily answered numerous questions on his equipment and methods and we felt that readers would wish to share his additional information.

The lathe and chuck used by the author were specially made to his own design. Such lathes are powered by motors varying

between 1/3–1 hp and run between 800–1200 rpm, although for the heavy turning described in his article the speed was 350 rpm.

To ensure that the tools are cutting precisely on the centre plane line, the professor projects the image from a halogen lamp slide projector throughout the turning process. The slide is easily produced by scratching through the emulsion of an over exposed or over developed section of black and white film a single straight horizontal line.

Oval turning is no more dangerous than straightforward circular turning, but, as you will see in several photographs, Professor Volmer wears a glove as a safeguard. He also advocates the use of goggles or a face protector.

For the design of objects with elliptical cross-section, the creative designer has one dimension more than the turner of round pieces.

This article originally appeared in *Woodturning* issue 5, Autumn 1991.

Fig 2 Perspective views of the oval bowl rotated around its vertical axis in steps of 22.5°

Elm platter, rim V grooved,
200mm x 25mm (8in x 1in)

Spalted willow hollow vessel,
underside grooved,
200mm x 90mm (8in x 3½in)

Yew platter, rim grooved,
230mm x 30mm (9in x 1⅛in)

Cherry platter, rim grooved,
200mm x 25mm (8in x 1in)

Simple ornamental turning

How you can use a router to produce decorative flutes and grooves that will give your turnings the ornamental look

W. T. Hughes

While I was still working, a friend loaned me four of the original Holtzapffel volumes on ornamental turning and his lathes, with the comment 'There's nothing new in turning'. It was heavy going reading through those volumes. A few years later, having a copy of *Ornamental Turnery* by Frank M. Knox, my interest was renewed in the results of ornamental turning, but not the desire to carry it out.

This year, when doodling to come up with patterns to embellish bowls and platters, the answer came, 'Why not use a router?' By a simple method it should be possible to put straight lines on the sides of bowls or across the face of a platter.

My current router, an Elu Mof 96, has twin 10mm (⅜in) diameter guide rods with which to set the cutter distance from the guide block. If, instead of locking the guide rods to the router base, they are fixed rigidly, and the router moved along them, a horizontal plane can be achieved.

Tool rest holder

A rod having a tight fit, and long enough to be at least 60mm (2⅜in) higher than the centre point of the lathe headstock, is fixed vertically in the tool rest holder. Two holes are drilled in line in the rod, at a position equidistant from the centre point of the headstock, to take the guide rods. In my case I measured the holes to be 85mm (3¼in) apart centre to centre (see Fig 1).

Both ends of the guide rods have now to be threaded, one end to accept a single nut, the other, two nuts plus the diameter of the vertical rod. When fitting the router assembly to the vertical rod, and locking the guide rods with the two nuts either side, it can be

held firmly, while being able to slide along the guide rods, the single nuts acting as a stop.

Horizontal cutter

You now have a horizontal cutter that can be positioned on, above, or below the centre point of the lathe headstock.

In use I find that the guide rods flex. To correct this, an 'L' shaped block of wood is fixed to the open ends of the guide rods by the single nuts. The foot of the block is clamped to the lathe bed.

Index head

Last and most important you need to make an index head if you haven't one already.

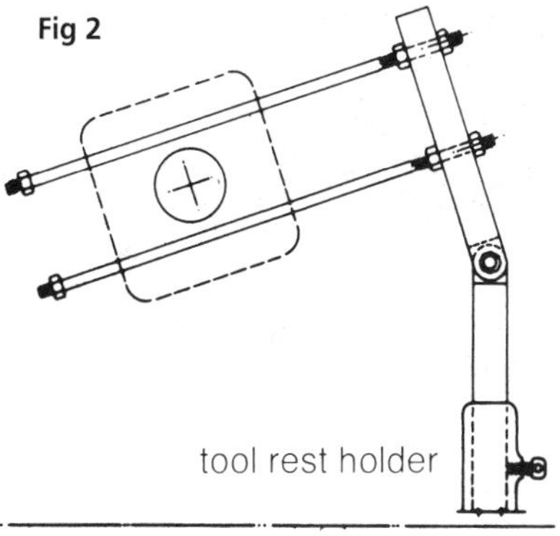

Tool rest post

The next thinking was 'Why not have straight lines in planes other than horizontal?' To achieve this, a tool rest post was cut in two and half-butt jointed with a locking nut and bolt (see Fig 2).

The same length tool post rod as before can be used if cutting with the router angled upwards. When used in a downwards angle, a longer tool post rod is required. Because the commencement of the cut is above the centre line of the headstock in this configuration, it is necessary to raise the tool post rod in the holder.

If your tool post holder is straight and clear at the bottom, only one tool post rod will be required. Mine is swan-necked, being on a Graduate short-bed lathe.

So far the router cutters used have produced decorative flutes and grooves. (Some examples are shown in the photographs.) Using parallel-sided cutters, grooves can be cut truly. They can then be filled with contrasting inlay strips . . . and the field of use widens.

This article originally appeared in *Woodturning* issue 6, Jan/Feb 1992.

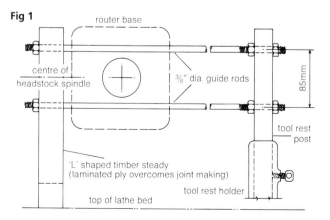

Fig 2

tool rest holder

Fig 1

router base

centre of headstock spindle

⅜" dia. guide rods

85mm

tool rest post

'L' shaped timber steady (laminated ply overcomes joint making)

tool rest holder

top of lathe bed

Stickwork for use in woodturning

You will never look at off-cuts in quite the same light once you have read this chapter describing the techniques and fascination of segmented turning.

Dick Bew

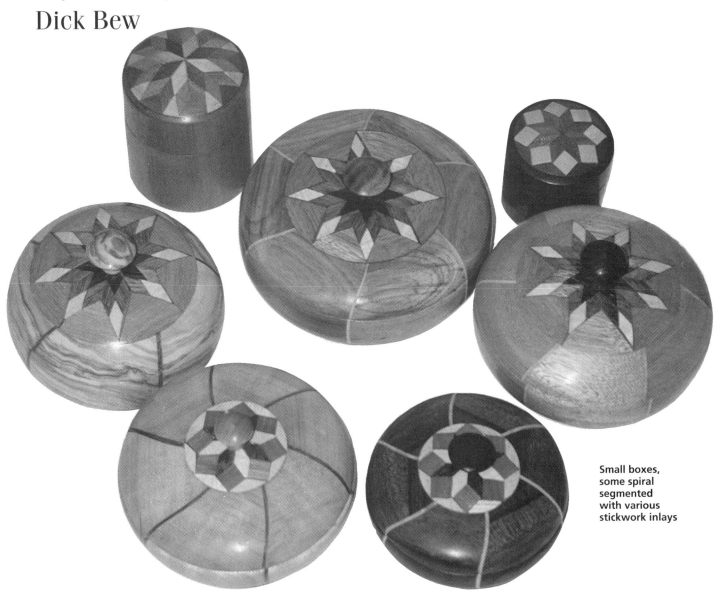

Small boxes, some spiral segmented with various stickwork inlays

Stickware has been produced for many years as a form of inlay decoration for wooden items. It was well known in the nineteenth century in the Tunbridge Wells area, where it was often called Tunbridgeware and later developed into wooden mosaicware.

I have adapted stickwork to enhance turned items particularly, to brighten up a plain piece of wood and add another dimension to wood turning. I have used it to good effect in coasters, tablemats, boxes and dishes, and centres of segmented wine tables. Much of my turning is segmented work, to save wood, and the off-cuts from this are often suitable to build up stickwork blocks.

The basic principles

Stickwork is made by gluing together different coloured woods in lengths, or sticks, to form pleasing geometric patterns. Each pattern is made up from three main shapes, or combinations of them – diamonds, triangles and squares, which are glued together to form an end pattern. When dry the block is then turned into a cylinder. Slices are taken off the end and used as a decorative inlay. Depending on the thickness of the slice this inlay can be shaped on the lathe into convex or concave shapes to suit the piece to be decorated.

Let's have a look at some of the simpler patterns:

a. Diamond shapes cut at 30° will give a rather 'spidery' 12-pointed star, but, infilled with triangles, I have found it works well for the centre disc of a clock face (Fig 1).
b. Diamonds cut at 45° give an eight-pointed star and infilled with other shapes can be most effective (Fig 2).
c. Diamonds cut at 60° give a six-pointed star, but if they are arranged into hexagons you have a tumbling block effect (Fig 3).
d. Triangles cut at suitable angles can be built up to form octagons or hexagons and added to as required (Fig 4).

The number of patterns you can design are unlimited. Ideas can be obtained from books on marquetry and parquetry. However, do not make them too complex at first, because they have to be cut out in short-grain sticks of wood and built up. This can become very tedious if a large number of different shapes are used.

General requirements

Apart from a lathe you will need a band saw and a thicknesser. Some form of mechanical sanding is helpful but not essential.

1. Band saw showing mitre guide with stock upright slicing diamonds. Fence to blade distance set at length of diagonal cut. Additional stock and cut diamonds on the right

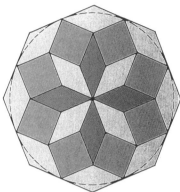

Fig 1 Diamonds cut at 30° give a 12-pointed star infilled with 60° triangles make a suitable disc for the centre of a clock face.

Fig 2 Diamonds cut at 45° give an 8-pointed star and infilled with squares produce an interesting pattern.

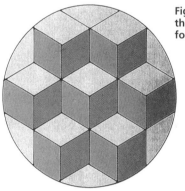

Fig 3 Diamonds cut at 60° then arranged into hexagons form a tumbling block effect.

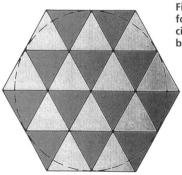

Fig 4 Triangles cut at 60° and formed into a hexagon. Thin circle line shows turning between centres.

To make sticks take pieces of contrasting coloured woods between 230mm (9in) and 460mm (18in) long, between 75mm (3in) or 100mm (4in) wide and thickness between 5mm and 10mm (⅕in and ⅜in) (my thicknesser only measures in mm). It is very important that all pieces are the same thickness; if you have diamonds with small differences of thickness you will not be able to build up an accurate pattern.

Say we decide on 60° diamonds, use a band saw with the widest blade having at least 8 tpi (teeth per inch). The finer the better for ensuring a tighter fit without too much cleaning up and sanding. Set the mitre guide at 30°, place your selected stock upright against the mitre guide and slice off the end across the grain to give a 60° angle on the end of the stock.

The length of this diagonal is the blade to fence distance. This length will vary with different angles and thicknesses. The length can be calculated, but I find it easier to measure it after the first cut. Set the fence at this distance from the blade, slide the wood on the mitre guide up to the fence and cut your first diamond. Now check to see if your sides are equal. If not, adjust the fence to get it right. When you are happy, slice off your diamonds by pushing the wood up to the fence each time, having calculated the number of diamonds you want beforehand and adding a couple for breakages or bad shapes (Photo 1).

To make triangular sections, set your mitre guide to the appropriate angle and your blade to fence distance equal to the base of the triangle. Cut your first angle and turn your stock over 180°, push up to the fence and slice your first triangle, turn again, and so on until you have the right number. For squares the thickness of the stock will differ. Used in conjunction with 45° diamonds, its thickness should be the same size as the diagonal. With the mitre guide set at a right angle and the fence-to-blade distance set at the thickness of the wood, you then cut your short-grained square section. Your stock this time lies flat on the band saw table.

Wall clock showing 30° diamond stick work inlay for centre disc

If you really want to drive yourself up the wall, instead of preparing your stock of one type of wood, you can glue up, say, seven thicknesses of different veneers, suitably selected for varying or alternate contrasting colours. When dry, you can now cut this composite piece of stock into either diamonds, triangles or squares. These shapes need to be cleaned up after cutting on the band saw. Some woods take more cleaning up than others. The finer the teeth and the sharper the blade the cleaner the cut. I use a belt sander with 120 grit, but be careful not to alter the angle.

Having removed all the rough edges it is time for gluing up. The type of glue I now use is aliphatic resin glue. This is like a PVA but has better heat-resistant qualities, which improves sanding; it tends to run and drip less; and the stickwork disc is less inclined to move or creep as much once shaped on the lathe, as it does with a normal PVA glue. Setting time is about 15 minutes at normal temperatures. You can use super glues or epoxy resin glues to save time, but they are expensive. Hot hide glues could also be used but they are not so convenient as the PVA type.

To hold the shapes in place, while you build up the block to allow

the glue to set, use elastic bands, top, bottom and centre on a 100mm (4in) stickwork block. Allow the block to dry overnight before turning on the lathe. It is also important that the grain in the outside shapes all goes in the same direction. If it does not, when you come to turn between centres to produce the cylinder of stickwork, the gouge will dig chunks out of those shapes with the grain running the other way.

We now have a stickwork cylinder block from which we can slice

2. Component parts for making up a stickwork block of 45° diamonds and squares

discs with the band saw for inlay decoration; the thickness of the disc depends on what you are going to use it for. For flat surfaces such as coasters and tablemats 2 – 3mm (⅛in) is ample. If a curved surface is required, say for a rounded top box lid, then 8 – 10mm (¼ – ⅜in) should suffice. If you want stickwork on the lid of a box to have both curved surfaces on the inside as well as outside, then 15mm (⅝in) may be better.

You may often get small gaps between the stickwork pieces once you have made up the block and it has dried out. This is more likely in larger blocks with a diameter of 150mm (6in) and above. Don't worry about filling in these gaps until later. Slice your disc off, insert it into the workpiece and shape it on the lathe. Go as far as sanding down to 180 or 240 grit. Stop the lathe and have a good look at it. If there are any small gaps, use wax filler sticks of the nearest colour, melted or rubbed into the gap. If there are large gaps, say up to 1mm, mix up the appropriate sawdust with epoxy glue and use that as a filler. A point to remember is that the smaller the original shapes are, the smaller the gaps and the less likely they are to show.

Building up 45° diamonds and squares

Start by making an eight-pointed star. Take two contrasting woods, sycamore and purpleheart. Cut 12 sycamore and four purpleheart 45° diamonds. Clean them up as before. Take one purpleheart piece, glue along the end grain side and fix to a sycamore side grain. Make up four pieces in this way. When dry, glue up these four pieces, two at a time, to form the star.

3. Stickwork block of 45° diamonds and squares built up and held with elastic bands for the glue to set

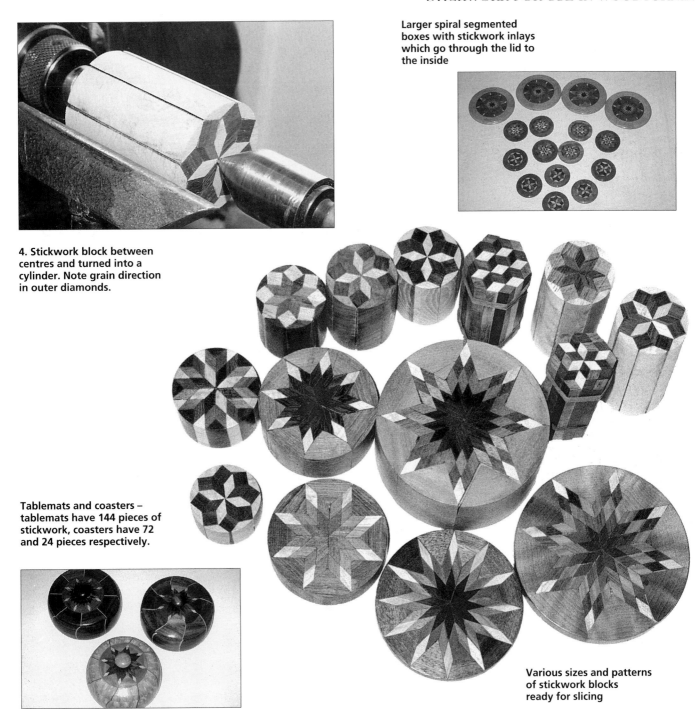

4. Stickwork block between centres and turned into a cylinder. Note grain direction in outer diamonds.

Larger spiral segmented boxes with stickwork inlays which go through the lid to the inside

Tablemats and coasters – tablemats have 144 pieces of stickwork, coasters have 72 and 24 pieces respectively.

Various sizes and patterns of stickwork blocks ready for slicing

See that the sycamore abuts to the purpleheart. Secure with elastic bands, making sure the centre points line up, and set aside to dry (Photo 2).

When the glue has set enough, clean out the valleys of surplus glue and fill them with contrasting square sections, in this case padauk. These square sections should be the size of the diagonal of the diamond; or each square can be built up from four half-size contrasting square sections to the full size. You will need eight squares to glue into these valleys. Again clean off the excess glue

and apply the remaining eight sycamore diamonds around the outside. Do make sure the grain in these outside diamonds is running all in the same direction (Photo 3).

If we had started with 8mm (⁵⁄₁₆in) stock for the diamonds, the squares would have 10mm (⅜in) sides, and the end resulting block of stickwork would have a diameter of 50mm (2in) and be 100mm (4in) long after turning between centres (Photo 4).

This cylinder block of stickwork is ready for slicing and inlaying into your turning; the application of this will be dealt with later.

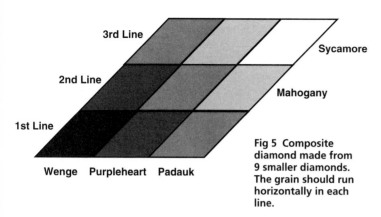

3rd Line

2nd Line

1st Line

Wenge   Purpleheart   Padauk

Sycamore

Mahogany

Fig 5 Composite diamond made from 9 smaller diamonds. The grain should run horizontally in each line.

Building up larger star patterns

To produce larger stars (see Photo 5) the same principles are used in making the simple eight-pointed stars already described, but the difference is in the way the 45° diamond is made up (Fig 5). This is made of nine smaller diamonds, and formed by three diamonds long by three diamonds wide, graded in colour from one point to the other. Five contrasting woods are needed.

Depending on the size of the block required the 'composite diamond' can be made up from the smaller diamonds, e.g. 4,9,16, 25 etc. Sixteen small diamonds, original stock size of 6mm or nine small diamonds of 8mm stock width will give an approximate diameter of 125mm (5in). I keep mine to just below 150mm (6in) diameter as that is the maximum size I can slice off on my band saw.

When planning the basic design there are several points to consider: (a) the final diameter, (b) the number of small diamonds and the width of stock, (c) the number of contrasting woods, (d) the number of diamonds from each type of wood.

To clarify this see Photo 6. The star is made up from composite diamonds each containing nine smaller diamonds of 8mm (⁵⁄₁₆in) stock, a total of 72 small diamonds divided into five contrasting woods.

The table below shows the number of diamonds for each wood starting with wenge at the centre and working out to the point of the star with sycamore.

For 16 small diamonds per composite diamond you need a total of 128 small diamonds from seven different woods. For 25 then 200 small diamonds are required. With the larger numbers you

may be running out of different coloured woods. This can be overcome by repeating part of the sequence, or holding the small diamonds loosely in your hand and arranging them in the colours you find most effective.

So we have cut and sorted our diamonds into the pattern we wish to create; now we build up our composite diamond, line by line, using the example in the table. For the first line glue wenge, purpleheart and padauk together and set aside to dry. Follow this with the purpleheart, padauk and mahogany line, and then the final line, padauk, mahogany and sycamore. A simple gluing jig helps.

Now glue the lines into the diamond composite block by taking the first and second lines, apply glue to one surface and line up the 45° edges and check colours are aligned correctly. Use clamps to hold together. Take the last line, glue, align and clamp to the other two in a similar way.

6. 8-pointed star made up from composite diamonds

7. 12-pointed star made up from composite diamonds consisting of four smaller diamonds. Suitable for a clock face

This is where it can become a little tedious; you need eight of these composite diamond blocks. They are glued up two at a time, making sure they align properly. You now have four pieces: glue these up in a similar fashion to complete your star, and hold in place with elastic bands. Make sure the centre is lined up, and set aside to dry.

We have our large star, but instead of filling in the valleys with squares, we use right-angled triangles. The triangle's two sides must be extended to enable a complete circle to contain the points of the star (see Fig 6). The grain of the triangle must run parallel with the longest side.

Cut eight triangles, fit them into the valleys, numbering each and the corresponding valley. Mark off where the points of the star meet the triangle sides. Draw a line 67.5° to the longest side to meet this mark and cut off the waste

position	centre	2nd row	mid row	4th row	point	totals
wood type	wenge	purpleheart	padauk	mahogany	sycamore	5
no. diamonds	8	16	24	16	8	72

Composite Diamonds

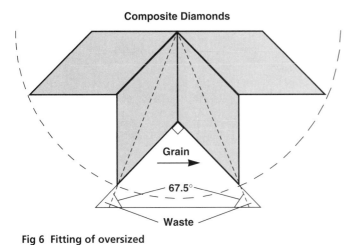

Fig 6 Fitting of oversized right angled triangles into valleys of 8-pointed composite diamonds

pieces on the bandsaw. Make sure each modified triangle fits snugly into its valley, adjust on the belt sander for a perfect fit if required. Glue these triangles into opposite valleys, two at a time, holding both in place with one clamp. When all eight triangles are fitted, and glued, mark out the largest circle possible on the end of the block and bandsaw your blank into shape before finally turning on the lathe.

You now have a cylinder about 150mm (6in) diameter 100mm (4in) long ready for slicing off your stickware inlays. For flat surfaces like coasters you should get 36 inlays between 2mm and 3mm thick.

Extending the diameter

To make your stickwork inlay larger, say for the top of a wine table

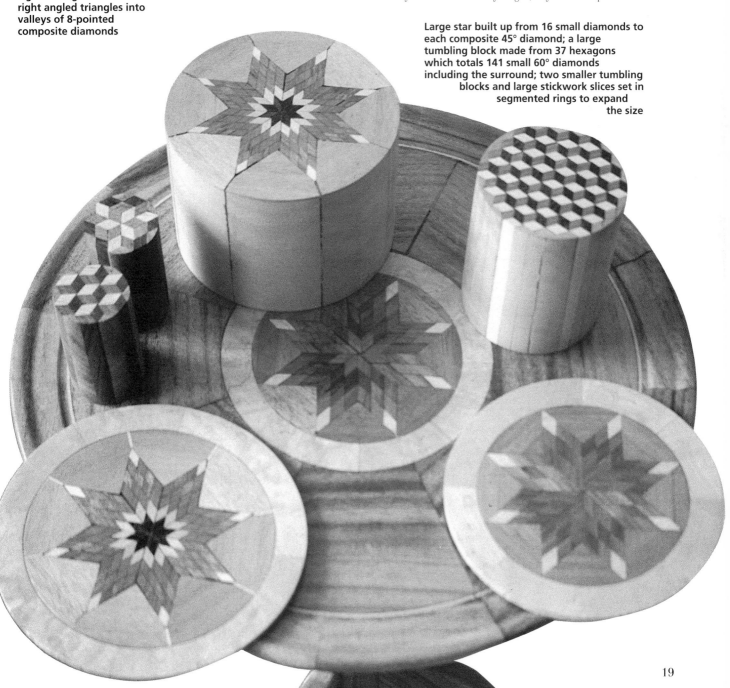

Large star built up from 16 small diamonds to each composite 45° diamond; a large tumbling block made from 37 hexagons which totals 141 small 60° diamonds including the surround; two smaller tumbling blocks and large stickwork slices set in segmented rings to expand the size

8. Wine table showing expanded inlay in the top of the table

9. Stickwork inlayed into a segmented ring to expand the size

10. Expanding the size of the inlay by inserting into a segmented ring

11. Tumbling block effect using 7 hexagons and 6 diamonds for the surround

(see Photo 8), and where you are restricted by bandsaw size, you can make up an eight-segmented ring in a suitable wood to the required diameter, glue it up and turn on the lathe. Set your 150mm (6in) diameter stickwork slice into this segmented ring (see Photos 9 and 10). To make sure the stickwork inlay is stable in the ring, I fill the underside of the inlay with fibreglass filler. When set, sand off to a flat surface on the underside.

Tumbling block patterns

To produce a tumbling block effect you require three different woods, shaded dark, medium and light, together with another contrasting wood for the surround. For an eventual stickwork block of about 38mm (1½in) diameter you will need seven 60° diamond sections, stock width 6mm (¼in), in each of the three woods and six for the surround. In my example I have used wenge, padauk and sycamore with a bubinga surround. Prepare these 60° diamonds as described before. Take a stick of each, and glue them together so that the grain runs in a circle, i.e. always end grain to side grain. (See Fig 7).

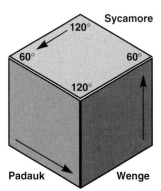

Fig 7 Making up hexagons from three 60° diamonds. Arrows indicate the grain direction, i.e. always running in a circle

It is very important to assemble the pieces in this way to achieve a uniform grain and colour to get the tumbling block effect on completion. Glue and bind the sticks together using elastic bands and leave to dry.

We now have seven hexagons. Take one and glue the remaining six around the sides of the first one. Make sure that the sycamore, in this case, is always at the top of each hexagon. Finally fill in the surround with the six bubinga diamonds, remembering to keep the

grain running in one direction. Centre carefully on the lathe and turn into a cylinder (Photo 11).

Expanding the tumbling block

To increase the diameter of the tumbling block pattern is not straightforward. A hexagon will fit into a circle and the radius of the circle equals the diagonal length of the diamonds making up this hexagon. The width of the hexagon, i.e. the distance between any two parallel sides, is shorter than the vertical distance, i.e. the diameter of the circle. Therefore, grouping a large number of

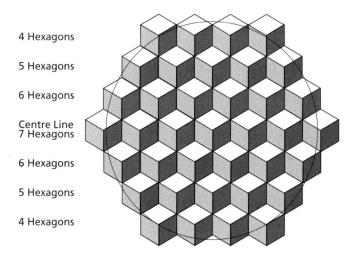

4 Hexagons

5 Hexagons

6 Hexagons

Centre Line
7 Hexagons

6 Hexagons

5 Hexagons

4 Hexagons

Fig 8 Tumbling block effect using 37 hexagons. Maximum diameter shown by dotted line

hexagons together to make a circle is not possible without cutting through parts of the hexagons at the circumference. The easiest way to understand this is to draw it. (See Fig 8.)

To make a tumbling block of about 90mm (3½in) diameter, make up 37 hexagons as before. Group seven along the horizontal centre line with sycamore at the top, build up six more hexagons above and below the centre line, followed by five and then four hexagons

12. 6-pointed star expanded to form a double tumbling block effect

in a similar fashion making seven lines altogether. Glue these up and hold with elastic bands. When the glue is dry, draw the largest circle on the end of the block. Cut this on the band saw into a cylinder as accurately as possible to reduce the work on the lathe.

We now have the problem that some of the grains around the circumference will be going the wrong way for turning on the lathe. To overcome this, centre up accurately on the lathe, run at medium speed and, with a drum sander in a drill, sand to a perfect cylinder.

Another method used to build up a different formation of tumbling blocks with 60° diamonds is to start with a six-pointed star and expand outwards (Photo 12). This has a double tumbling block effect. This type can be enlarged by adding on additional 60° diamonds, but again it is easier to follow if you draw it out beforehand.

Uses of stickware in woodturning

I have used stickwork inlays in coasters, tablemats, various types of box including spiral segmented ones, platters, dishes, bowls and tops of wine tables to name a few. The photographs should give you some ideas.

The advantages of stickwork over veneered inlay is that you can shape it on the lathe to give curved surfaces both convex and concave. You can use the standard lathe tools for cutting, although you may find a scraper more efficient to blend in the stickwork with the surrounding wood before sanding.

The disadvantages are that it can take a long time building up these blocks, and it can get very tedious if you over-complicate the pattern. However, the end result is very satisfying.

This article originally appeared in two parts in *Woodturning* issues 6 and 7, Jan/Feb 1992 and March/April 1992.

13. Inlay inserted in a spiral segmented box showing convex shape on lid

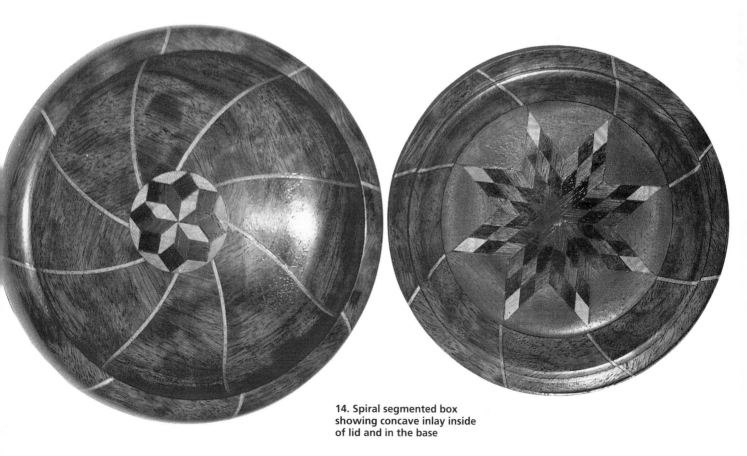

14. Spiral segmented box showing concave inlay inside of lid and in the base

Lenticular leanings

How a chance remark about turning knife blades led to the development of a fascinating technique which involved mathematics, sketching, trial runs on the lathe, thinking up wheezes and devising widgets

Geoff Heath

I t was my privilege to give the opening lecture to my local branch of the AWGB (High Peak Turners) on 'Widgets and Wheezes', describing the gadgets and techniques I had adopted for solving some of the problems we all encounter in the workshop. After the lecture, one of my fellow members commented that I seemed to be more interested in *how* to do the job than in actually *doing* it. Whilst not agreeing with this assessment, I must admit that I prefer to sit down with pencil and paper before picking up a chisel and attacking a piece of wood.

Now that the branch is in full swing, members are asked to turn a small item for display and comment at each meeting. Recently, we were invited to make a paper-knife.

Several members at once asked 'How do you turn a knife blade?', to be told that it was possible to turn a square between two consecutive pairs of centres, thus producing intersecting arcs which would form a lenticular section (Fig 1). This left me wondering, 'How far apart should the centres be to produce a given profile?' A little trigonometry and a few simple calculations soon gave the answer. They also gave me some ideas for further developments.

Fig 1 also shows the relationship between the principal dimensions such as the width and thickness of the blade, the radius of the 'swing', the distance between centres and the angle subtended by the blade. It is clear from this diagram that

$b = R \cos \alpha$
$w = R \sin \alpha$
$t = R - b = R(1 - \cos \alpha)$
whence
$w/t = \sin \alpha/(1 - \cos \alpha)$
$R/w = 1/\sin \alpha$
$b/w = 1/\tan \alpha$

By choosing suitable values of α, it is a simple matter to construct Table 1 with a pocket calculator.

The values of w/t, R/w and b/w are plotted against α in Fig 2. Let us now look at a simple example in the use of these curves.

Suppose we wish to make a blade 25mm (1in)

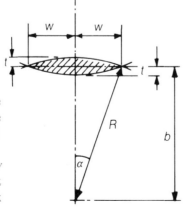

Fig 1 Geometry of a lenticular section

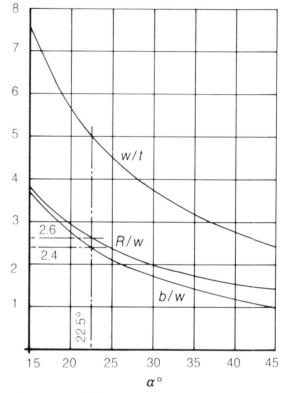

Fig 2 Curves of w/t, R/w and b/w versus α

Table 1						
α deg	sin α	cos α	1 -cos α	w/t	R/w	b/w
15	.2588	.9659	.0341	7.59	3.86	3.73
20	.3420	.9397	.0603	5.67	2.92	2.75
25	.4226	.9063	.0937	4.51	2.37	2.14
30	.5000	.8660	.1340	3.73	2.00	1.73
35	.5736	.8192	.1808	3.17	1.74	1.43
40	.6428	.7660	.2340	2.75	1.56	1.19
45	.7071	.7071	.2929	2.41	1.41	1.00

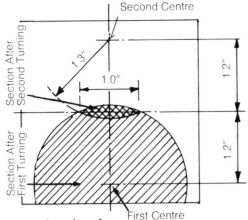

Fig 3 'Two-centre' turning of a knife blade from a square block

polygonal prism, thus restricting the choice of values for α, and hence of all the other parameters.

1. Octagonal block with blade blanks attached

Some more mathematics (with which I will not bore my readers, beyond saying that it involved the solution of three simultaneous equations by means of a simple quadratic) enabled me to derive the width/thickness ratios which could be obtained using regular polygonal prisms with between four and eight facets (See Table 2).

Now a practical width/thickness ratio is about 5, which is why I chose this value for the above example. The nearest values of w/t to 5 in Table 2 are 4.781 and 5.385, which are obtained by using a heptagonal and an octagonal block respectively. The heptagon would pose some manufacturing problems, but an octagon is very easy to make. Having reasoned thus, I resolved to try an octagonal block, and, if this did not work, I would resort to the hexagon, despite its thicker blades. The following paragraphs are based on my experiences after making this decision.

wide with a w/t ratio of 5. Fig 2 shows us that we must set α at 22.5°, giving b/w as 2.4 and R/w as 2.6. Converting these non-dimensional parameters into actual lengths by multiplying by w (= 0.5in), we obtain

$$b = 1.2in$$
$$R = 1.3in$$

In other words, we must set our two turning centres at 1.2in either side of the centre-line of the blade, and turn the workpiece down to two intersecting radii of 1.3in (Fig 3). This would result in a blade 1in wide and 0.2in thick, and would require a workpiece initially approximately 75mm (3in) square in order to accommodate the driving centre in safety.

As the blade took shape, the tool would make contact with the workpiece for a brief moment only once in every revolution, and I felt that this method would thus cause considerable 'knocking', which would not be conducive to a good finish. Moreover, a long blade of these cross-sectional dimensions would be very 'whippy', and it would not be possible to support the blade with a 'steady' or with the fingers, due to its non-circular shape.

The axis of the blade would not coincide with the line between the centres, so the pressure of the tailstock would bend the blade unless a strut was placed between the centres to resist this pressure as the thickness of the blade was reduced.

My block is 255mm (10in) long and about 55mm (2¼in) across flats, each of which is 25mm (1in) wide (Photo 1). In order that the block could be re-used, I thought it best to attach the strips by screws, drilling oversize holes in the strips to

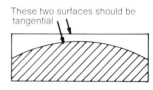

These two surfaces should be tangential

Fig 4 Section of blade after first turning

allow for any small discrepancies in dimensions. A round-headed screw with a washer under the head ensures that the strip is well clamped. The screws should be positioned close to the extreme ends of the strips, care being taken not to approach these areas with the cutting tool during turning. I used a skew chisel for the flat portions and a wide, shallow gouge for the run-outs.

It is important that the first turning does not cut an arc which falls inside the original surface of the blade blank, especially at the ends (Fig 4).

If this happens, the block will be unable to support the strip properly during the second turning, resulting in vibration and bowing, thus producing a variation in both thickness and width along the blade. It is therefore desirable to leave a very narrow

Faceted block

While thinking about providing such a strut with lateral extensions to support the half-finished blade, I hit on the idea of a faceted block on which would be mounted several 'blade blanks' in

Table 2	
No.of facets	**w/t**
4	3.000
5	3.588
6	4.181
7	4.781
8	5.385

the form of thin strips of wood. The outer surface of each strip would be at the correct radius from the axis of rotation, and the strip would be supported along its entire length by the block. Not only would this eliminate virtually all the 'knocking', but it would be much more economical in wood! However, I foresaw limitations to this method, since the block would be in the form of a regular

2. Blade blanks ready for mounting on the block

3. Circular end of octagonal block. The facets were made tangential to the circle.

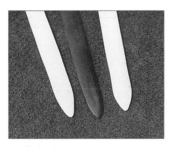

4. Original design of tang

5. Blade tips

6. Finished paper knives (holly) of original design

7. Revised design of tang – now reduced to a peg

'flat' on the crest of the blade during the first turning to ensure a good 'seat' when the workpiece is inverted.

The strips should be prepared (Photo 2) with their width and thickness as near as possible to the final dimensions of the blade so that (a) there is a minimum gap between the strips, thus making for smoother turning, and (b) when inverted between turnings, the centreplane of the blade is in the correct location relative to the surface of the block. Having said that, it is nevertheless preferable to have the strip too thick rather than too thin. This may result in a slightly oversize radius for the first turning, but the error will not be noticeable.

My octagonal block was not made quite as accurately as I would have wished, and any errors in its shape were compounded by further errors in positioning the driving and revolving centres. Even minute dimensional errors were a large percentage of the thickness of the blade, and manifested themselves by one blade (or, in some cases, one end of a blade) being turned down to the required shape before any of the others.

In order to 'fine-tune' the block, I turned a 3mm (⅛in) wide circular section at each end, making sure that the two circles were of exactly the same diameter, with at least one facet tangential to one circle, the other facets standing proud. The block was then rubbed down on a sheet of abrasive paper until all the facets were tangential to the circular ends (Photo 3).

Small variations still occurred in the thickness of the blades, since all my blade blanks were cut on the bandsaw and then rubbed smooth. Despite the improvements to the block, the thicker blades still reached their desired profile before their fellows. Once a blade had achieved its required shape, I was obliged to remove it completely, thus enabling the other blades to be reduced without taking more off the surface of the blade in question. Regrettably, this brought on some 'knocking' which increased as the number of blades remaining was reduced. However, short of putting all the blade blanks through a thicknesser (which I don't possess), I decided that this was the simplest method.

8. The 'nose' of the handle after turning. Note that the rest of the handle is left square to simplify cutting the slot.

When all the blades were finished on one side, they were inverted and replaced on the block, and the turning process described above was repeated. During the second turning, the criterion for a blade being ready for removal is the state of the edge, which has to be sharp and straight so that a true lenticular section is produced without reducing the width of the blade.

Wood

The success of the method depends to a large extent on the type of wood which is used for the blade blanks. Obviously, a hard close-grained wood is preferable; holly and ebony worked well, and I had some good results from oak, which I thought might splinter along the edge. But the best results came from a piece of quarter-sawn plane (lacewood) which not only turned superbly, but also presented a beautiful pattern along the blade. Now I come to think of it, the oak was quarter-sawn, too, which may be the key to a good finish with no edge-chipping.

Having turned the blade, I had to find a way of fixing it into a handle. After removing the portions containing the screw-holes, one end was cut into a 'tang' (Photo 4), which was worked down to a circular cross-section by 'screwing' it through a series of holes in a steel plate, so that it could be glued into a hole drilled in the handle. The shoulders on each side of the tang were cut away, and the tip of the blade was carved to a point (Photo 5). The blade was finally rubbed down with abrasive paper to remove any minor imperfections, and the complete knife was finished with a sanding sealer and wax polish (Photo 6).

The base of the tang was the weak spot of this design since, for a 25mm (1in) wide blade, it had a circular cross-section of only 5mm ($\frac{3}{16}$in) diameter. Table 2 shows that the values of w/t for the octagon and the hexagon are in the ratio of 1.287. Bearing in mind that the stiffness of a circular section is proportional to the fourth power, and its strength to the cube of its diameter, we find that the tang of the 'hexagon blade' is 2.75 times stiffer and 2.13 times stronger than the 'octagon blade' of the same width and the same material. In deciding whether to stay with the octagon or change to the hexagon, I had therefore to balance considerations of the strength and stiffness of the tang against the slenderness of its section.

Since I was biased towards the octagon-blade, what was obviously needed was some local reinforcement of the joint between the blade and the handle. This was achieved by cutting a slot in the handle, and leaving a longer unturned portion at the handle end of the blade, thus providing a 'flat' which would fit snugly inside the slot. The tang then became merely a short peg (Photo 7).

A new problem now arose. The best stage at which to cut the slot was before the handle was turned, i.e. whilst it still had a 'face and edge' which could be easily located against the table and fence of the band saw. This would not only have made

9. The nose after slotting

10. A 'widget' to support the handle after slotting

11. The widget in use, enabling the slotted handle to be turned

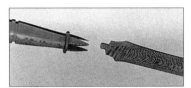

12. A blade ready for fixing into its handle

the slotted section too flimsy to turn, but would also have removed the material which would provide a centre!

'Wheeze' and 'widget'

Some further thought provided a 'wheeze' and a 'widget' to solve this problem. The blank 125mm (5in) long x 20mm ($\frac{3}{4}$in) square – for the handle was mounted in the lathe, and drilled centrally 5mm ($\frac{3}{16}$in) diameter to accept the peg on the blade. The 'nose' portion which would contain the slot, together with the bead adjacent to it, were turned and finished completely, using the 5mm ($\frac{3}{16}$in) hole as the location for a revolving centre (Photo 8), whilst leaving the remainder of the workpiece square. The nose was then slotted on the band saw (Photo 9), a stop being provided to control the depth of the slot. Each handle was 'tailored' to be a good fit on its own blade.

A piece of scrap was turned to a cylinder about 25mm (1in) diameter and 75mm (3in) long, and bored out 15mm ($\frac{5}{8}$in) diameter and 25mm (1in) deep at one end to accommodate the nose. A hole drilled in the base of this recess allowed an old 5mm ($\frac{3}{16}$in) drill to be firmly bonded in place as a mandrel (Photo 10). The workpiece was then pressed on to this drill until the bead of the handle was hard against the lip of the recess. The handle was then re-mounted in the lathe (Photo 11), and the turning completed.

Whilst still in the lathe, the handle was rubbed down, sealed and polished. After removal from the lathe, the driving end was cleaned up by hand. The blade was then glued into the handle (Photo 12) and the finished knife (Photo 13) was given a coat of paste wax before being polished with a soft cloth.

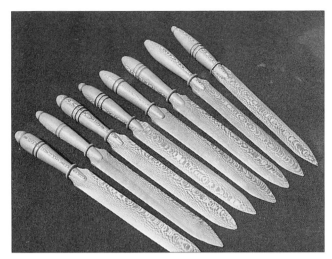

13. A set of finished paper knives (revised design) in lacewood

14. The tapered octagonal block

fact that the handle is in line with one face of the blade rather than with its centre-plane, are features which are neither obvious nor of any consequence (Photo 17).

So, from a chance remark about turning knife blades, I developed a fascinating technique which involved mathematics, sketching, trial runs on the lathe, thinking up wheezes and devising widgets. Much more fun than churning out bowls!

This article originally appeared in two parts in *Woodturning* issues 6 and 7, Jan/Feb 1992 and March/April 1992.

15. Tapered blade blanks being mounted on the block

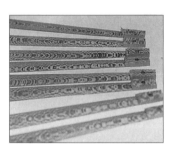

16. Tips of tapered blades after the second turning. Note the excess thickness.

17. A set of finished lacewood paper knives with tapered blades

Octagonal block

Having mastered the techniques of blade making and handle fixing, I decided to look into the feasibility of an octagonal block in the form of the frustum of a pyramid, which would produce tapered blades. My new block was also 255mm (10in) long, with facets which tapered from 22mm (⅞in) to 10mm (⅜in) (Photo 14). Again, much of the work of making the block was done on the band saw, final tuning being achieved with a plane and a sandpaper block, although there is no need to get a smooth finish – where the 'as sawn' surface is at the correct level, it is best left alone.

The blade blanks (Photo 15) were tapered in plan, but not in thickness. This not only made the blanks very simple to produce, but ensured that there were two parallel faces at the butt end which would fit snugly into the slot in the handle. The extra thickness at the tip, coupled with the need to keep the turned surface flush with the unturned end, meant that the radius of curvature of the surface at the tip after the first turning was slightly greater than desired. When the blade was turned over, the second turning had to allow for this extra thickness, more material being removed at the tip than at the butt. Apart from these considerations, the tapered blades were made in exactly the same way as the straight variety.

Photo 16 shows the lop-sided appearance of the tip after the second turning. However, once the unturned area is removed, the difference in curvature between the two sides of the blade, and the

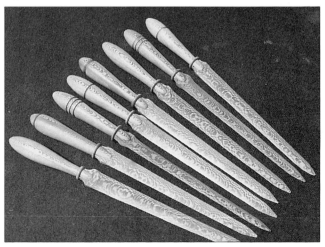

Thread cutting in wood

How old-timer Kevin Rosetta realised a lifelong ambition to cut threads in wood

Terry Martin

The current boom in woodturning has attracted a lot of new hands to the craft, but there are still a lot of old-timers around who can show us all a few tricks of the trade. Australia is no exception. Many a backyard workshop around the country houses a 'living national treasure' who has forgotten more than most of us will ever know.

One of these turners is Kevin Rosetta of Brisbane in Queensland. Kevin, who is now 69, started turning at the age of 13 on a second-hand treadle lathe with a home-made concrete flywheel. At 18 he

progressed to another, larger treadle lathe and started making fishing-rod handles and reels. After the war he put a half-horsepower motor on the lathe and installed it in his new workshop under his house. He had a job with a fishing-rod manufacturer and worked both in the factory and in his own workshop at home. Any good turner will tell you that production work is the way to increase speed and accuracy, but Kevin adds that turning on a treadle lathe taught him how to cut efficiently. He retired in 1981 but never lost his love of turning.

A visit to Kevin's workshop is to enter a veritable Aladdin's cave of woodturning tools spanning over 50 years of the craft. Kevin's skills as a wood machinist enable him to make a lot of his own equipment. This article is about one of his recent projects and is an example of how to make precision machinery with a minimum of cost.

Kevin had always wanted to cut threads on wood, but lacked a cross slide for mounting the cutters. After reading the article in the Winter 1990 issue of *Woodturning* about Bonnie Klein's thread-cutting machine, he decided to make his own version. Kevin made up a frame from craftwood and mounted a second-hand dentist's drill motor in it. This motor runs at 7,000 rpm (Photos 1 and 2).

Sequence

The sequence for making a threaded box on Kevin's machine goes like this:

1 & 2. Kevin's home-made thread-cutting machine

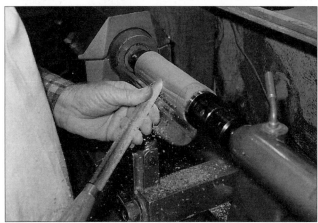

3. Kevin mounts a blank on his lathe with a chuck at each end. The wood in this case is Deep Yellow Wood, particularly suitable as it is dense and clean-cutting. One end is a threaded cup chuck and the other is a collet chuck, which happens to be what Kevin had available. Kevin then cuts a cylinder to a good finish.

4. Next he parts the cylinder into lid and base sections. Because they are already mounted in their chucks, they are guaranteed to line up later. Yes, the tool is a normal size – Kevin just happens to have rather big hands!

5. Kevin then trues up the end of the lid, which is the first section he will finish.

6. Hollowing the lid using a back-cut

The thread cutter shown in the photos was ground by Kevin from an old router bit. He hand-ground it with two teeth, thus effectively doubling the cutting rate. This of course requires a steady hand when grinding as the two teeth must match to cut a smooth thread. This problem is eliminated with a single cutter, but there is a 50 per cent loss in cutting rate. He has also ground a smaller cutter from a 6mm (¼in) twist drill for getting into narrower apertures.

Details of Bonnie Klein's thread-cutting machine can be obtained from Klein Design Inc.

This article originally appeared in *Woodturning* issue 7, March/April 1992.

7. Further hollowing using scrapers

9. Measuring the internal diameter to size – 50mm (2in) in this case

8. Further hollowing using scrapers

12. Kevin then feeds the lid in with the 16 tpi feed screw while the cutter cleanly cuts the thread.

13. The base is then dimensioned on the lathe for its thread cut.

15. The lid is then removed from its chuck, screwed onto the base and the top is finished off on the lathe.

10. A final stepped cut to 52mm (2¹⁄₁₆in)

11. The lid is mounted on the screw cutting machine. The cutter, home-made, is lined up with the edge of the wood to be cut and the small sliding scale, seen just to the right of the box, is set to zero. The motor cradle is then wound in 1mm, which sets the depth of the screw cut.

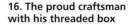

14. The outside thread is cut on the base. The handle on the right feeds the cutter into the wood.

16. The proud craftsman with his threaded box

Adapting plain lathes for ornamental turning

You do not need to be vastly wealthy or a mechanical genius to start OT. Here's how to get going with a few home-made adaptations.

Mike Foden

Holtzapffel and Evans are names revered by ornamental turners everywhere, and it is pleasing to note that over the past couple of years ornamentally turned work has gradually appeared in exhibitions, magazine articles and books. Most of the woodturning fraternity shy away from the idea, believing that expensive antique equipment and tooling is necessary to decorate plain turnings, but be assured that this is not so.

The cross slides and cutter frame

The complete apparatus set-up

I started woodturning as a hobby some eight years ago, and, after producing spindles, bowls and small boxes for three years from every conceivable timber, I decided that there had to be something else worth exploring. Having exhausted all designs of boxes, I needed some further enhancement to make them more attractive, apart from the colours and grain patterns of exotic timbers.

Division plate

Not having heard of ornamental turning, I was intrigued to see some ornamental turning work in a display case during a turners' open day at Alan Holtham's. Shortly afterwards I read an article which mentioned ornamental turning, and although no work was illustrated I did learn that a cutting frame and division plate were required as basics. These can be obtained from Chronos Ltd of St Albans for little more than the price of a screw chuck, and are superbly engineered.

I did, in fact, make my own division plate, which was quite accurate, but as I became more proficient, I bought a professionally made plate. The chuck that holds the plain turned item, when screwed up tight on the spindle nose, will hold the division plate securely, and a detent of spring steel arrests the work at measured intervals, enabling the cutting frame to remove segments which ornament the work.

Division plates are available with various numbers of holes and with a centre bore to fit any lathe spindle. Most of my work is ornamented using a 96-hole plate as this will produce ample combinations.

Frames

Although there were many types of cutting frames available in the past, I believe that the only ones made commercially today are those from Chronos. I have found the 100mm (4in) cutting frame to be ideal in the horizontal mode, and the 50mm (2in) frame works well as a vertical cutter.

To drive these frames an overhead is required, which on the true ornamental lathe is a massive affair. My overhead is a 20mm (¾in) steel bar 510mm (20in) long secured vertically in the lathe saddle – or

**These long-stemmed vases were
turned from old ivory billiard balls**

the cross slide if an engineer's lathe is used. Although the Coronet Elf has provision for this bar (in the hole intended for the travelling steady), the new Coronets will need to be adapted to suit.

Even though the Elf was notoriously difficult to set up for ornamental turning due to the single round bed bar, I did manage to produce gallery quality turnings for almost two years on this lathe. I now have a Myford ML10 engineer's lathe for the

ornamenting, although much of the basic work is still undertaken on the Coronet.

The vertical bar is drilled through near the top for a 10mm (⅜in) steel bar and the latter is fastened to a Dremel tool holder. This holder clamps the Dremel motor tool securely, and the entire set up swivels like a universal joint, and moves along the lathe bed with the saddle or cross slide.

Blackwood box with silver inlay

**Box made from blackwood,
partridgewood and silver**

Patterns turned using the eccentric cutting frame

A small pulley is placed in the Dremel collet and this drives the cutting frame via its own pulley. If an intermediate set of pulleys on a bar is interposed between the motor and the cutting frame, the system becomes much more versatile.

Cutters

Now we come to the cutters themselves, which are basically fly cutters. Initially I struggled for months before producing a successful cutter and I still make my own by grinding high speed steel pieces (often obtainable as offcuts from router bit manufacturers).

The many cutter profiles are shown in Holtzapffel vol. 5, which

is essential reading if you intend to pursue this type of work. It is hard going in places as it is written in precise Victorian style, but there is a wealth of information which cannot be found elsewhere. You will have to ignore many of the photographs, as the Victorians went over the top with ornamentation, often embellishing every part of their work with patterns.

When making the cutters be sure to grind plenty of clearance all round so they will not wedge in the work. The cutting edges must be polished after being ground to shape – a medium India stone followed by a hard Arkansas will do the trick. Details of a Goniostat (jig for stoning the correct angle on the cutter) are to be found in Vol 5, and a simple version is easy to make and use.

The cutting frame is held in a tool clamp and this is a simple matter if an engineer's lathe is used. However, you will have to do a little juggling if you are adapting a woodturning lathe. I originally purchased two Emco topslides and bolted one on the other at right angles, and secured the cutting frame in these.

The lathe tool rest is removed and the slides, which are supported on a stem underneath, are secured in its place.

Apart from the drive belt, which is approximately 2mm (3⁄32in) round section and endless (for availability see *Yellow Pages* under 'Rubber Manufacturers'), this represents the entire set-up.

Plain turnings

We now come to the production of the plain turnings, which have to be completely finished and polished before they are decorated. I do not propose to detail the making of a simple lidded box, but would stress that you will find it easier if all the surfaces to be decorated are formed of perfectly flat planes, although it is possible to ornament curved surfaces as you become more

Blackwood, pink ivory wood and silver box

Blackwood and tulipwood box

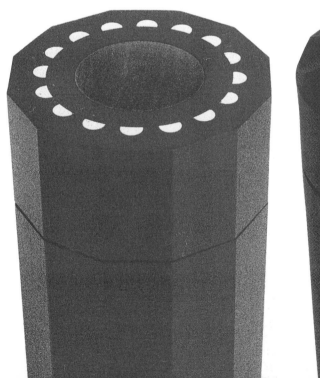

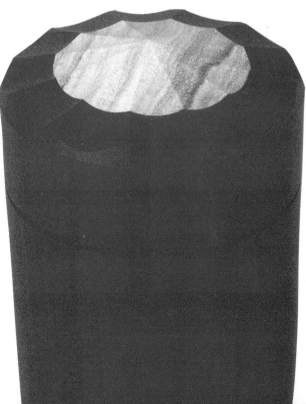

experienced.

The ideal material for this work is ivory, and, although I still use old ivory (e.g. billiard balls) for some work and inlays, it is far too costly to use regularly, apart from being ecologically unacceptable to many people.

There is only one really suitable timber and that is African blackwood. Good quality African blackwood can still be found, albeit in small sections, but it is difficult to obtain the quality that was available 30 years ago.

There is no point in ornamenting colourful exotics with beautiful grain patterns as the ornamentation is lost in the figuring. A plain surface is necessary, and, apart from blackwood, you may care to try partridgewood, boxwood or purpleheart, although it is blackwood that should give the finest results.

Choosing good quality wood is a matter of experience and this will only be acquired by trial and error over a period of time. It should be mentioned that it is not possible to polish the finished pattern other than with a little wax on a soft bristle brush held in the Dremel. This means cutters must be sharp enough to impart their own polish to the wood, and this they will if sharpened and polished correctly. (The Goniostat is essential for this.)

Eccentric

There is one more cutting frame that is useful and can be made on a metal turning lathe by anyone proficient. This is the eccentric cutting frame which will be found most useful for making circular patterns on box lids (details again from Holtzapffel vol. 5).

I made my own after only six months of self-taught metalwork and it has proved to be perfectly accurate and reliable during four years of regular use. However, if you don't feel confident enough, contact AB Engineering in Tunbridge Wells for a quotation.

Finally, if you do get bitten by the OT bug, you must join the Society of Ornamental Turners. The members have a wealth of experience between them, and I have found them most helpful especially in the early days when I regularly telephoned around for information.

Although I now know what I am doing it took a long time for everything to fall into place and this was, I suspect, because I live in a part of the country bereft of ornamental turners. There was no chance of hands on experience and everything had to be learned from books. However, perseverance has paid off, even though I have often remained in the workshop until the early hours of the morning trying to solve problems.

In a single short article I can do no more than scratch the surface of such a vast and involved subject and I leave it to the reader to make further investigations into this most interesting and intriguing pursuit.

This article originally appeared in *Woodturning* issue 8, May/June 1992.

Box made from blackwood, partridgewood and silver

Blackwood and tulipwood box

Texturing, finishing and colouring

The techniques Merryll uses to create the subtly textured and coloured pieces for which she is known

Merryll Saylan

Part 1: Texture

Thank goodness, I thought, texture's spelled the same, unlike color/colour, the subject of part 3 of this article. I'd finally learned how to pronounce words like tomatoes, bananas, half; buy my wood by cubic foot not board foot, call it timber and not wood. No less deal with spelling like-sounding words, and then what happens, I go back to the US. Never mind, though I used to say 'Oh, well', I think 'Never mind' is a better expression.

I decided that before I discussed how-to-do-it, it would be better to talk about what the word/term means, why and how you might use it, design considerations using it, and then some tools and methods I use.

Texture refers to the surface of a material, to its character, its structure. It is perceived primarily through touch, the surface feel of a piece. Smooth is as important as rough. Materials have texture; wood itself has texture. Texturing creates contrast, changes the feel, creates tone. Tone refers to the quality of colour, shadow and brightness, light and dark. Texture is also perceived by that contrast and tone.

When designing a piece incorporating texture/texturing, there are several ideas to consider. Try to visualise the piece, in its entirety. What is it that you want? The elements must work together; there should be some consistency within the piece. Since texturing creates contrast, how do you want to work with dark and light, shadow? Are you decorating the surface or superimposing something on it? Are you enriching the surface? Are you embellishing it? Many a beautiful piece has been ruined by inappropriate decoration. Either the form is enhanced or it probably should not be there.

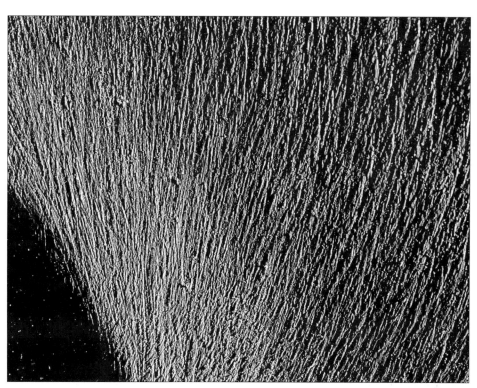

Texture can be directional, with strokes, marks, gouges, scratches, all used to enhance the direction of a shape. It can be applied all over the surface of a piece or limited to some area such as the rim. Texture can be static: punching, dabbing, spotting, used to enrich a surface. Study of the world around us, of nature, architecture, materials, opens us up to ideas. Doing rubbings on surfaces, sketching with a soft pencil on soft paper, trying textures on scrap wood – all increase our awareness, our vocabulary of texture.

In visualising texture, there is another very important concept to consider. Part of the process of texturing is the preparation of the surface for its final finish, its final appearance. When I sand a piece smooth, in addition to the way I want the piece to look and feel, I prepare it for its finish. When I add texture, I am also preparing it for the particular finish I have chosen – it may be an oil-rubbed finish, it may be for colour, or lacquer or a waterbased

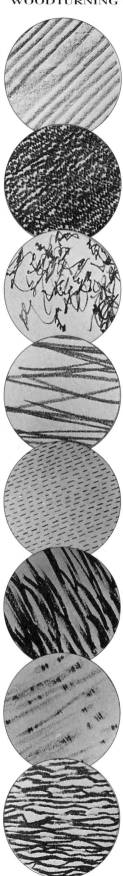

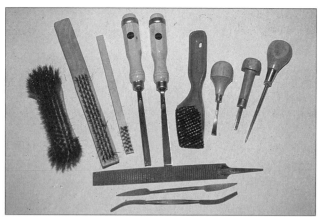

Various hand tools that could be used for texturing

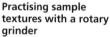

Practising sample textures with a rotary grinder

product such as bleaching. I will talk about this more in parts 2 and 3 of the article.

'An artist is ever cognizant of this infinite variation in all existence and therefore feels impelled to exercise variation in his work . . . His constant search is like a continuous journey through life, the ending of which would be less pleasant than its continuation.' Kenneth F. Bates

Tools

There are many, many tools you can choose from to create texture – from hand tools to power tools. Hand tools could include carving tools, files, rifflers, surforms, wire brushes, coarse sandpaper. Lathe tools such as beading tools and diamond points can be used successfully to make grooves, lines and ridges for texture. The two power tools I use primarily are the rotary (die) grinder, air and

electric, and the angle grinder. The rotary is used off the lathe with the piece mostly finished before carving. The angle grinder I use both on and off the lathe. My tendency is to use anything that will give me the result I'm after. Try one – if not satisfied, try another.

The rotary grinders work on the principle of a rotating burr carver, with a collet holding the cutting bit. There are many varieties on the market, with some incorporating both a mechanism for reciprocating carving (duplicating the action of a mallet and chisel) as well as the rotating head. Some have a flexible shaft attached to a motor of some sort, some have variable speeds and reversing ability. Reversing would be quite an advantage when dealing with wood grain direction, and where the angle of approach and accessibility might be difficult. I'll discuss that a bit further on.

Some small rotary tools are now available with 'quick change handpieces' eliminating the problem and annoyance of changing collets or locating chuck keys. There is a huge range of prices and some of the least expensive are quite good. I would recommend getting variable speed; one for the control it gives you but also different accessories work better at different speeds; carving burrs require high speed, sanding flaps and wire brushes do better at fewer rpm.

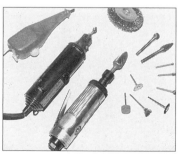

Air grinder, Dremel engraver and various burrs, brushes for texturing

Diamond point lathe tool being used to cut grooves

Pencil studies of texture

Accessories

There is a surprising range of accessories for these tools with burrs available in steel, high-speed steel, carbide and recently a burr consisting of needlelike barbs of tungsten carbide. There is also a great variety of drum and flap sanding attachments, abrasive points (stones) and more.

The rotary grinder can be used for removal of material as well as applying texture. I recommend practising on a sample board various techniques and burrs. Try deep biting cuts, bouncing cuts, tapping the surface. Pay attention to grain direction and how it affects cutting or whether there is tear out. Excessive pressure during use can bend or even break a collet, mandrel or cutter. Never over-tighten the collet. Minimise overhang of the bit to prevent bending shafts.

The patterns the burrs carve seem directionless. In actuality the way you cut, the angle the tool approaches the surface creates a direction and changes the pattern, tone, light and dark. To understand that, because it will affect the appearance of the finished piece, take a sample board, carve a fairly large section in one direction, turn the piece around and carve another section adjacent to the first. Then turn the piece another quarter turn and carve one more section.

This is where the reversing tool might be handy. Let's say you're carving the surface of a large flat platter with a slight bowl shape. It is pretty awkward to carve the whole surface from one approach unless, of course, your body is capable of contortion; mine would

Close-up of Dremel and tear-out from burr

protest. Usually, you will have to turn the piece. Understanding the directional change in the pattern the burr leaves will enable you to design for it, perhaps following the grain pattern, however you think it looks best.

Protection and safety

For both types of grinder, the rotary and the angle grinder, there is quite a lot of dust and particles flying about. Always wear protection for face and eyes as well as having dust collection. If you are carving for long periods of time, hearing protection would be wise. Since the rotary is used off the lathe with the piece fairly well finished, consideration of the base, how to secure firmly while carving, whether the piece will need to be remounted after carving, should be thought through. You want both hands on the tool. In a hurry, I have tried using my elbow as a clamp, but you end up spending more time – or making serious errors – while trying to save time. Clamps with padding to protect the piece is one solution; that trusty third hand, the hot glue gun is another.

I use the angle grinder primarily on the lathe with the work revolving. It works similarly to power sanding only it is far more powerful and turns at much greater rpm. It is fairly lightweight and compact for its capabilities. I use mainly coarse sanding disks, 100–125mm (4–5in) diameter, 24–36 grit. (Disk sizes vary even from the same manufacturer in my two countries. I used a 90mm (3½in) disk while in England, only to be told upon my return to the US that there was no such thing.)

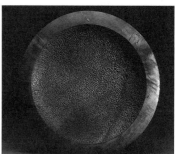

North Sea, platter, maple wood, 510mm (2in) height x 510mm (20"in) diameter. Finished piece with overall carving by rotary grinder

Detail of carving *North Sea*

Angle grinder, safety shield, side handle and sanding disks

Angle grinder texturing rim

When I use the sanding disks, I've removed the guard which gets in the way. With the other accessories available for the grinder, such as the chain-saw type carver, metal cutting wheels, wire brushes, or the new carver with the needlelike carbide barbs, NEVER, NEVER, use the grinder without the safety shield on and the side handle attached. Even sanding disks can be dangerous and you must always keep your hands and fingers well away from the rotating disks.

Experiment

As recommended for the rotary grinder, practise with the angle grinder on waste boards to get used to the operation of the machine and accessories. Experiment to see what kind of textures you can achieve. Do not forget to fix the board you are working on. Try a waste piece on the lathe. The arc of the disk determines the pattern you get. You are only touching the surface of the wood with a small portion of the disk. Different patterns result from an even, slow sweep of the tool from the centre outwards or small arching patterns as you work from the centre to the rim with short scallop-type movements.

It seems as if the tool could be used to carve a lot of material away and compensate for turning errors, a lumpy surface or tear marks. All usually read through when you apply your finish or run your hand over the surface. It is far better to prepare the piece for the texturing with proper turning techniques. Turn a clean surface with smooth curves using your scraper. All you will then need to do is take one or two passes with the grinder to achieve your texture. An exception might be for a piece with a thin rim. If the piece has warped, has any movement or flex, one or two passes might not do it – especially if the piece is turning out-of-round. It will take a bit more work, care, and passes.

Sometimes it seems pretty foolish to clean up a surface carefully with those lathe tools and then set about scratching up the surface with that 24-grit paper. But heck, that rough texture is what we're after.

The angle grinder is a loud and powerful machine. Don't be afraid of it but do use it with respect. When working with both machines, one last reminder: if the grinder runs smoothly when it is not under load but does not run smoothly under load, you are using too much pressure. It is never necessary to force it, the weight of the machine by itself is adequate. Forcing and too much pressure can cause problems, particularly on those thin out-of-round rims.

Recently I've been learning how to use a computer. I have high hopes for what it will do and the time it will save me. My son reminded me that it will not solve all the problems I may think, that it is just another tool, another machine. It only does what I want it to do.

Birches, detail of rim

Birch amongst the Larches, Grizedale, platter, plane wood, 38mm (1½) height x 380mm (15in) diameter. Rim textured with angle grinder

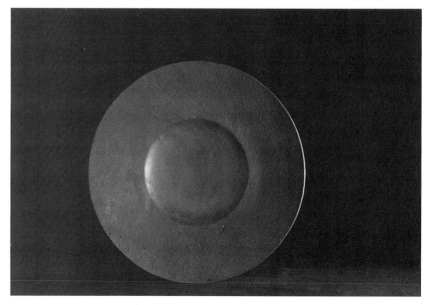

Part 2: Ebonising and bleaching

I had been dyeing bowls black for sometime when I attended a two-day workshop with Wendell Castle at a local art school. During a slide lecture Castle showed a piece of furniture he said was made of ebonised oak. I wondered if ebonised was different from dyeing something black. I came away with the impression that it was. Upon further reflection, I came to the conclusion that I was ebonising. Yup – that's what I was doing.

Developing a philosophy that there are many routes to get somewhere helps to work with these materials. Each method has its good and bad points, each has different qualities. Variations may occur even using the same material on different woods. This can sometimes make the decision of which one to use and on what, a hard-to-define, subjective decision. Experience and preference will help make the choice. Besides, I always prefer a loop trail when hiking on the fells. Who'd want to go up and back the same path?

The three mahogany plates: bleached, natural, dyed

Safety precautions

Protective gear

I noticed while living in England that there was great concern for the hazards of dust and protection of our lungs. In the States I felt less concern for that, though that's rapidly changing, but far more knowledge about the hazards of finishing.

Many of us worry about our environment and air quality, and rightly so, but less about ourselves. California has some of the strictest requirements in the US for finishing products, with many new products available. I've not been back long enough to really know much about them. Hopefully, these new requirements to protect the air will protect us. I'll try wherever I can to clarify differences in our finishes that are based on our countries' different requirements or even on the names we may call them.

In using any finishing, bleaching or colouring products you need to be aware of possible health hazards and use the appropriate precaution. Commercial finishes may contain toxic substances that can be absorbed into your bloodstream, not only through vapours, but also absorbed through your skin, or by inadvertently ingesting them while eating or drinking in your workshop. It's advisable to work in a well-ventilated area, outside perhaps – difficult in some places like the rainy Lake District. A proper finishing room would be best but not always achievable.

Wearing a fume/vapour respirator is important. A particle dust mask will not work and air-assisted helmets work only if they are equipped with a cartridge specifically for organic vapours. Respirators are made in many different sizes and styles. Fit one to your face and don't just buy off the rack. I wore one for years, steaming up my glasses because it did not fit well, only to learn it was for a much larger face size than mine.

A rule of thumb is that if you can smell any vapour, the mask is not working and needs either a new filter or does not fit correctly. There are industrial safety supply houses which stock these items and can advise and fit you with the proper product. Read labels and see which finishes really need a mask. Wear gloves, though not all gloves will protect from all finishes. I've dissolved some. Vinyl surgical gloves are relatively inexpensive, available in sizes and quite comfortable to work in.

Many finishes are flammable and should be stored carefully in sealed containers, preferably in steel cabinets. Dispose of your rags carefully as oily rags are susceptible to spontaneous combustion. Store in tightly covered metal containers designed for that purpose, or else wet them, spread them out to dry and then dispose of them when dry. Just in my neighbourhood, two woodshops went up in smoke due to oily rags.

Tools and supplies

Once you start getting into fancy finishes you start acquiring and needing a great many small items – plus the place to store them! Spray equipment is a great asset to have but will not be part of this discussion.

You will need a collection of brushes. Brushes are categorised by their filament – natural, synthetic or sponge. Solvent-based products such as lacquers, shellacs and spirit stains are usually applied with natural filament brushes. Water-based products with synthetics, oil-based with either. Foam pads and brushes, difficult to find and expensive in England, are very good for stains but will dissolve in lacquer products.

Supplies

Choose the brush for the job you want, but the most expensive brush may not be the one you want. It is sometimes better to get an inexpensive brush and discard it after the job – it is frequently cheaper than using solvents to clean the brush. I found very high quality brushes in England, some of which are unavailable in the US, but difficult to find them as inexpensively as the throwaway brushes I'm used to.

A good brush can last for years if properly cared for. Clean it in the solvent used to thin the material you applied with it. Get a variety of sizes. I have tiny brushes for touch-up, fan-shaped for spatter effects and broad ones for applying stains.

Other items worth collecting include: wipers – stockinette rolls, white rags, towelling, t-shirting, tak rags. Fine sandpaper, wire/steel wool, Scotchbrite pads. A load of containers, bottles, jam jars and small tuna fish cans are useful and mixing sticks. Wire brushes are another valuable bit of equipment also available in many variations. The list is endless, with the most important being some place to store this rapidly growing accumulation of things.

Preparation

In part 1 I talked about preparation for the final finish. If a smooth texture is what we're after, we sand our piece finely. If scratches and or sanding swirls are in that smooth part, they show up like a sore thumb when stain is added. Layering colours, creating dark and light, shadow and roughness can be used to advantage because of the way it absorbs stain. Smooth and rough sections absorb both colour and finish differently. The rough sections will look darker. It's like staining a board: the end grain absorbs more and always looks darker than the rest of the piece.

Bleaching materials. Getting ready to do sample plate and board

Bleaching, water stains or any water-based product will raise the grain/fibres. Plan for that in advance by wet sanding a piece or wetting the surface and when dry, sand down the fibres prior to applying the water-based product such as bleach or stain. A surface with fine texture,

Bleached bowl, Western figured maple (Photo: R. Sargent)

bleached, would lose definition by fibres raised from the process. One solution is to wet the surface, wirebrush the texture and then bleach. You may still have to wirebrush after bleaching. Good results come from good preparation.

Wood bleaching

Bleaching removes colour from wood. It is used sometimes to achieve a more uniform colour and for removing dark streaks on timber. Bleaching can help decrease fading or colour change of wood. Bleached surfaces will darken when exposed to light but the change will be minimal compared to unbleached wood. Ultraviolet absorbers added to a finish would slow even that down.

Safety considerations are very important when bleaching: wear gloves, goggles, apron and dust mask when sanding surfaces after drying. In general, the milder the bleach, the less the bleaching action and the milder the bleach the less the hazard.

The two most common chemicals used are sodium hydroxide (caustic soda, lye) and hydrogen peroxide. Most bleaches are two-solution, two-application bleach. The first part dissolves and floats colour deposits to the surface. The second part bleaches the deposits. I recommend commercially available bleaches. Follow the instructions carefully. Dispense only as much of the solution as you need, discarding what you don't use. Use separate brushes and mark for 1 and 2 containers. Use only plastic, glass or non-porous containers.

Neutralisation is the third step, though some commercial bleaches are self-neutralised. Neutralisation stops the action of the bleach, removing residue from the chemicals. It is an important step and if not done can cause problems with the

Mahogany plate. I turned three of the same mahogany plates to use as demonstration of bleaching and dyeing.

Applying part 1 of the bleaching process. Dissolving the colour, even staining the normally clear liquid from the lifted colour

Results on our sample figured maple plate and maple board

finish. Neutralising materials are usually acetic acid (vinegar) or oxalic acid.

Steps in the neutralising process are:

1 Wash the piece with cold water.
2 Wash with recommended acid.
3 Let stand for 15 minutes and then rinse with water.
4 Dry, usually overnight.
5 Sand to remove raised fibre and prepare for finish.

Good results come from good preparation

Drying of the surface is very important. The depth of bleaching may be as little as 1/1000in to ½in so you must sand lightly with very fine paper. I never use anything coarser than 320.

Bleaching seems to work better on warm, sunny days in the sunshine. The bright sun seems to add to the bleaching action, but a chemist told me it is the warmth and the reaction to that by the chemicals. In some commercial applications, the wood is heated prior to applying bleach.

Discolourations such as dark spots, mineral streaks, iron stains, glue stains, fungi or chemical stains are not adequately removed with the normal strong soda-peroxide solutions and other agents work better. Oxalic acid works well on iron stains and I was told of success bleaching out colour with a fully saturated oxalic acid and hot water mixture, but I didn't have any luck. Household bleach works on some stains.

You can purchase chemicals to make your own bleach, but it's easier to buy ready-made products. Here is one formula you could try. Required chemicals: Sodium hydroxide, hydrogen peroxide (28–35 per cent). Mix 4oz of sodium hydroxide with 64oz water. Apply the sodium hydroxide solution. Dry for approximately 30 minutes. Apply an even coat of hydrogen peroxide and dry. Neutralisation: follow steps from above.

Ebonising

There are several ways to achieve black. Choices are made on the kind of black intensity, the final finish required for the job, the difficulty of one application over another. The aniline dyes or stains are used the most. Anilines come in a variety of forms – spirit, water, non-grain-raising and naptha. Spirit is used the most frequently. In the US, spirit means 'denatured alcohol', in Britain it means 'methylated spirits'. I was told 'surgical spirit' could be purchased at the chemist's and is similar to what is used in the US.

Water stains should be dissolved in hot water; a little ammonia added helps penetration. Spirit stains work better warm, but since spirit is volatile, caution must be used for heating. I place a container in a pot of warm water. Buying spirit stain pre-dissolved saves you the

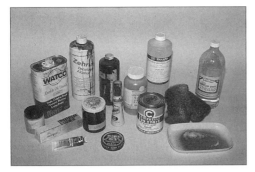

Ebonising materials

Applying spirit stain to sample mahogany plate

Service for two. Rice bowls and plates dyed with anilines and oil finish. Cabinet: satinwood and acrylic (Perspex). (Photo by Diane Padys, San Francisco.)

Chemical stain and sample board

Liam Flynn's piece, *Ireland*. Vinegar and iron stain on oak

problems of mixing. An overloaded spirit stain – supersaturated with pigment – put on cold will sometimes bronze. The alcohol goes into the wood, the stain stays on the surface.

The black stains sometimes have a bluish or purple tint which can be corrected to give you a truer black. I mix in a small amount of the darkest brown stain I can find. A friend uses a dark-walnut tinted oil finish for the first coat and that seems to take care of it.

Water stains will not be protected with an oil finish – shellac, lacquer or varnish-type finishes should be used. Spirit dissolves under some finishes that use spirit in them. I've had problems with brush lacquers.

Other ways to ebonise include chemical stains, vinegar and iron solutions, the charred or burn finish that Jim Partridge frequently uses. Garry Bennett, the well-known American furniture maker, uses black leather shoe dye applied in two coats and finished with a wax finish. Oil stains do not seem to dye as dark but can be

effective, and when used over other stains will deepen and add depth to the colour.

One of the darkest blacks is the one Wendell Castle uses. It is a chemical stain, a bit more troublesome to use but very intense.

Formula: Part 1 solution: 3½oz (100gm) copper sulphate, 1¾oz (50gm) potassium chlorate, and 22oz (615cc) hot distilled water. Part 2 solution: 3½oz (100gm) aniline hydrochloride, 1½oz (40gm) ammonium chloride and 22oz (615cc) hot distilled water.

Mix each solution in clean glass jars with tight fitting lids. Mix equal parts of 1 and 2 when needed, mixing only what you need for each coat. Apply three coats with a sponge or brush, allowing 24 hours drying time between coats.

The first coat goes on looking yellow, the second a little green, the third very green. When the third coat is dry, smooth it with fine sandpaper using oil as a lubricant. The oil will turn the stain a beautiful black. The oil could be tung oil, teak, linseed or any penetrating oil finish.

Vinegar and iron is very easy and most effective on oak and walnut.

Formula: 1oz (30gm) iron filings to 32oz (900cc) white vinegar (wire wool or/and nails can also be used but need to soak longer). Let the mixture sit for about a week. Strain through a paint strainer or several layers of cloth. Apply repeated coats until dark grey-black colour. Oil finish will bring it up to a deep black.

Part 3: Colouring

In the techniques and tools you might use for texturing, as well as for bleaching and ebonising, there is great variety. For colour, the list is essentially endless. You've decided to colour a bowl. How are you going to do it? Are you going to paint it? Do you want it to be bold? Are you trying to achieve something very subtle or do you just want to improve the natural colour of the timber?

Your decision as to what to use (and that decision will help determine how to use it), might simply be based on readily available materials. What do you already own? What can you borrow? What's inexpensive?

The decision may be made on the ultimate purpose of the piece: is it functional? What finish will it need? Do you want it to be dark or light, garish or delicate, flashy, arty, designed, organic, textured, smooth, uniform, gradated, transparent, translucent, opaque? Would you colour all woods?

Over the years, when displaying my work, people would come up, look at it, pick up a piece, shake their heads, and say, 'Colouring woods – nature didn't intend wood to be coloured. It's beautiful by itself. Why do you colour wood?'

There are some woods I would never colour. I don't use them very often. But, nature coloured wood – look at its many varieties

Recent coloured work by Liz and Michael O'Donnell. Mick told me they found some stains in a cabinet, did not know what they were, so just tried them.

and the range of hues. Some are very plain, and some beautiful. Adding colour will change the character of a piece. It can enhance the piece or simply call attention to itself. Painting, staining or dyeing pieces is really not that new.

This article is not long enough for a lesson in colour theory, but some terms are helpful. Hue is what we call a family of colours: a family of yellow colours, blue colours, families of dark or light colours, hues of warm or cool colours. Value is the lightness or darkness of a colour. Colour altered by white lightens the value and is called a tint. Black darkens the value and is referred to as shade.

Chroma or intensity of a colour refers to how saturated a hue is with colour, a colour of high intensity is brilliant, one of low intensity, greyish. In school we were taught that by using three primaries we could mix all other colours. In reality that's difficult to achieve. Several reasons are frequently given. One is that there are no pure primaries, another is the chemistry in paint and dye formulations.

Remembering that there is no single way to achieve a particular colour, experimenting is fun. And, for one-offs, it doesn't matter. It only becomes a concern when you need to replicate. Having a limited palette can be good training – mixing helps develop colour sense. A child's watercolour set would be good to start with and inexpensive. You can experiment prior to buying other materials.

The endless list of materials. You can colour wood with just about anything. Look what happens when you cut strawberries on a wooden cutting board. Stains and/or dyes are referred to by their medium – water, spirit, oil, varnish, wax. There are chemical stains and anilines, water pigment stains, synthetic dyes. I've also used fibre-reactive dyes, Procions, fabric dyes formulated for cellulose fibres. They are frequently used by basket makers.

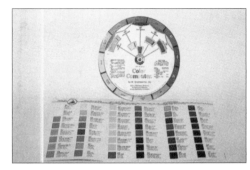

A colour wheel and card of commercial oil colours. The wheel aids colour mixing.

Pastilles. Pieces were bleached, dyed with a thin solution of fibre-reactive dye, then sealed with lacquer

Sycamore platter by Gael Montgomerie of New Zealand. Gael uses artists' acrylic paints for the speed and subtlety of watercolours but the permanence of oils.

A small collection of paint and colouring supplies

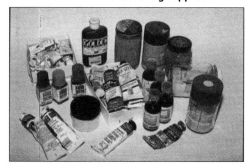

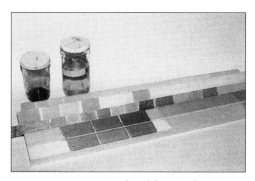

Sample Sticks. Needing to duplicate colours for commissions, I started making sticks. I begin with a saturated colour, dilute it in small increments, making notations on the boards of each addition for future reference. These colours are from fibre-reactive dyes, water based. I used the bleached board from the last chapter showing subtle differences in brightness between the bleached and natural timber.

There are all the paints and paint colours – powders, tempera paints, poster colours, artist's oils, watercolours, gouache, artist's acrylics, universal stainers or tinting colours, caseins. There are inks, markers, felt tip pens, shoe dyes and food colours. The list is endless!

As discussed in part 2, there are some basic rules worth remembering, regardless of the material or the method used:

1   Preparation of wood. Scratches, roughness, absorb colour. If you want a fine wash of colour, you want a fine finish.
2   Water stains raise grain. Prepare the surface before applying.
3   Natural wood has 'colour'. It affects your tint.
4   Finish adds colour. A dark oil finish will darken your colour. Sample boards help – natural wood, colour, finish.
5   Choice of finish: oil finish will not adequately protect a water stain. What will the function of the piece be, etc.
6   Colour changes from oxidation, just as does natural wood, but some paints change less than others. Check the product for colour-fastness.
7   Instructions: if you use materials not intended for wood, such as fabric dyes, instructions for its use will not be applicable. So it's trial and error. A good paint store with trained personnel may be able to answer some questions, and a dye supply house may also.
8   Problems: superglue will not take colour; it seeps into the pores and seals them. Epoxy, which can be tinted, seems to work better – of course knowing the final hue helps. Develop skills of the furniture restorer and touch up mishaps with paint and brush.

With perseverance and imagination, you can do anything.

These articles originally appeared in three parts in *Woodturning* issues 7, 8 and 9, March/April 1992, May/June 1992 and July/August 1992.

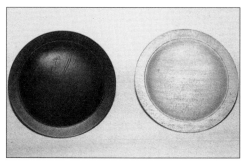

Sample mahogany plates: one ebonised, one bleached, with the turquoise oil coloured finish. This was unsuccessful on the bleached plate. Why? I broke my own rule and did not do a sample.

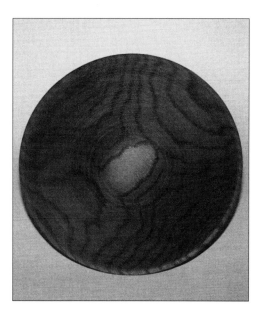

Oak plate with one coat of Danish oil tinted with black artist's oil colour. A second coat will enrich the surface. The black tones the garishness, fills the pores, and makes a more complex and rich colour. Layering colours, even using a tint of the same colour as the base stain in the finish, will enrich and add depth. When adding a colouring agent just be sure it is an appropriate medium for the finish.

Textured oak plate dyed red with spirit stain. It's pretty ugly at this stage.

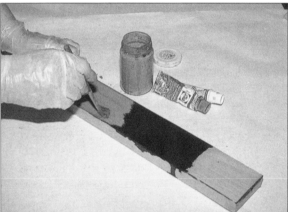

Applying turquoise oil stain to an ebonised sample board. This glaze and finish is a technique of adding artist's oil colours to Danish oil. Works most successfully on open-pore woods

Morecombe, Grizedale Collection, 50mm (2in) height x 460mm (18in) diameter. Purple oil glaze over padauk

Icefields, wall piece, 50mm (2in) height x 610mm (24in) diameter

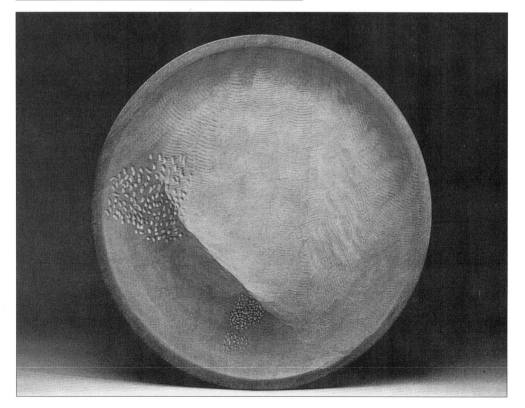

Widgets and wheezes

Some crafty ideas for making life easier on the lathe

Geoff Heath

As we gain experience in woodturning, we all discover more expeditious ways of doing things, so I expect that you, like me, make bits of equipment to make life easier. Since these are the things I'm going to write about, and since I like alliterative titles, I could have called this piece 'Equipment and Expedients', or even 'Gadgets and Good Ideas'. However, in my article 'Lenticular Leanings', I called them 'Widgets and Wheezes', so I'll adopt that as a heading. Well, it's held you so far, hasn't it?

No doubt some of the widgets and wheezes I am about to describe will cause some readers to say: 'That's obvious', or 'I've always done that', or 'That was in Keith Rowley's book'. But I trust that even if most of the ideas are old hat to some of you, a few of the ideas will be new to all of you. Not all of them are original, I must admit, but in most cases it was only after I'd invented them that I discovered someone else had beaten me to it!

Between centres

In order to look at things in a logical sequence, let's start where most of us start our turning – between centres. The simplest job is turning something from a square section. Now I know how the professionals do it – they bash a driving centre into one end, wind the tail centre into the other, and off they go with a roughing-out gouge, taking off the corners.

I have a bit more respect for my driving centre than to clout it with a hammer. Oh, I know what you're going to say – I should use an old driving centre as the punch. But the reason my old driving centres are pensioned off is because their corners have been chipped by occasional contact with a cutting tool. (I'll not mention how the tool fared in this encounter – but that was easily re-sharpened!)

Such a worn-out driving centre doesn't make indentations which are sufficiently long to provide a positive engagement for a pristine specimen, and if I lean too hard on the roughing-out gouge, I finish up with the driving prongs buzzing round on the end of the workpiece, after which I can't see where the true centre was.

Incidentally, one obvious wheeze is to make as many of the roughing-out cuts as possible from right to left, i.e. towards the headstock. In this way, the workpiece is pressed against the driving centre at the crucial time when the torque is at its greatest. But I digress.

Assuming the workpiece is more or less square in section, I set the fence on my bandsaw at half the width of the square from the blade, and just touch the wood against the blade to give a shallow slot. The wood is then turned through 90° to give another slot (Photo 1).

A centre punch is easily located at the intersection of the two slots to enable me to make a depression for the point of a four-pronged driving centre. This wheeze is particularly effective if there are a lot of identical pieces to turn, or when accurate centring is essential. Once the fence has been set, it's a very quick method.

I also like to make the squares into octagons before I start turning, especially if the section is more than 50mm (2in) square. Not only does this make the roughing-out process much easier, but it can yield some valuable pieces of wood – not necessarily for turning. A lot of mine end up as stakes for plants in the garden.

Do I hear you muttering about the difficulties of producing an octagon? There's really nothing to it. All you do is mark the diagonals on one end of the workpiece (you were going to do that

1. Square on band saw table after cutting shallow slots to ensure positive engagement of a four-pronged driving centre.

2. Square on tilted band saw table prior to removing the corners. Note inscribed circle on the end of the workpiece.

anyway, to find the spot for the tail centre), and use a pair of dividers to scribe as large a circle as possible.

The table of the bandsaw is then tilted at 45°, and the fence set so that the blade is just on the waste side of the circle (Photo 2). Once the fence is set, all four corners – and those of any other identical workpiece – can be speedily removed to leave a perfect octagonal shape.

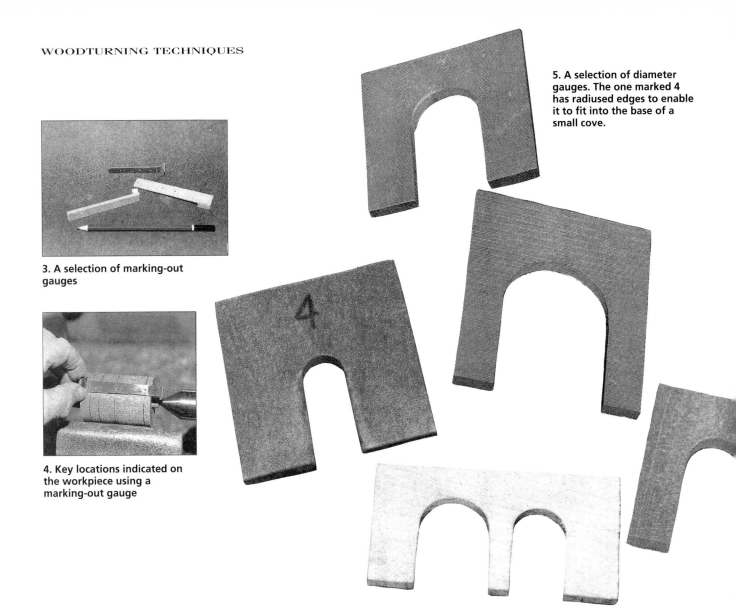

3. A selection of marking-out gauges

4. Key locations indicated on the workpiece using a marking-out gauge

5. A selection of diameter gauges. The one marked 4 has radiused edges to enable it to fit into the base of a small cove.

Marking out

If you are going to make a reasonable quantity of identical items such as door knobs or eggs, it pays to make two simple widgets. The first is the marking-out gauge. This is made from a thin strip – say 12mm x 3mm (½in x ⅛in) – of scrap wood (I have also used sheet brass) roughly the same length as the workpiece. To one end of the strip I glue a small piece of the same section (or just bend the brass) to make an end-stop or hook (Photo 3).

Using the inner face of the stop as a datum, I drill a series of small holes at key locations. First, I drill the holes right through the strip with a 1.5mm (1/16in) drill, and then (if it's a wooden strip) open it up to 2mm (3/32in) halfway through, giving an approximation to a tapered hole.

This widget is held against the cleaned-up end of the revolving workpiece, and a sharp pencil is poked into each hole in turn to indicate the location of important features (Photo 4).

The second widget is well known, and I take no credit for its invention. Instead of continually re-setting your callipers to check the diameter of the object at the critical points, you make a set of wooden gauges (Photo 5).

These are easily cut from a thin 3mm (⅛in) slip of scrap. If they are intended to check the diameters at the base of coves, their internal edges will need to be radiused.

Table legs

Despite what I said in an earlier paragraph, there are times when you must leave the corners on your workpiece – table legs are a good example. Here you need to retain the square section at the top of each leg so it can be mortised to accept the rails supporting the table top.

The danger is that while turning the rest of the leg, an accident will cause the corners to be taken off and the leg will be ruined. I have three wheezes to minimise this danger – all the results of unfortunate personal experiences!

The first wheeze is to make a shallow saw-cut around the leg just below the point where the square section ends. Again, the band saw comes in handy here, the rip fence being set so that the cut can be repeated in exactly the same place on all four faces of all four legs (Photo 6).

When the leg is being rough-turned, a long splinter is sometimes raised which would otherwise run to the end of the workpiece, taking off a corner just where you want to keep it on. But the saw-cut acts as a 'fire-break', and the splinter will not run beyond it.

However, even that wheeze will not prevent a carelessly handled tool from chipping a corner. How often have I withdrawn a tool sideways from the workpiece, only to be surprised when it hit the almost-invisible whirling corners. My next widget is designed to minimise this danger. It consists of four lengths of wooden angle section such as you can buy at any DIY shop. These are fitted over the four corners in the critical region (Photo 7), and strapped in place with masking tape.

A warning: don't use rubber bands. I did (once!) – and the centrifugal force stretched them sufficiently to allow the angles to escape and I was pelted with flying corner-protectors.

This widget needs to be slid back towards the end of the leg while you are cutting the chamfer between the square and the round sections. Despite the precautions I have described, this is when the square section is most vulnerable. You are cutting into the corners on the 'unsafe' side of the 'fire-break', and you have just pushed the corner-protectors aside.

The final wheeze is an insurance policy. It's simply a band of masking tape around the square at the point where the chamfer begins (Photo 8). It will not stop you damaging the corners, but it will retain the resulting chips and splinters so that they can be glued back into place!

Now let's look at another specific example of spindle-turning: captive rings on rattles and goblets. Dave Regester showed us how to make a baby's rattle in Issue 4 of *Woodturning*, and Maurice Mullins demonstrated the goblet in Issue 6. The trick is to shape the captive rings as completely as possible before they are parted

6. Cutting the 'fire-break' slot around the top of a table leg. Note the use of the rip fence to locate the slot at the correct distance from the top of the leg.

7. Corner-protectors in place on the table leg. The roughing-out cut has raised splinters, but these cannot run into the square section because of the 'fire-break'.

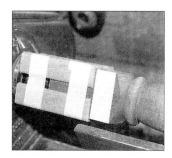

8. The chamfer and bead at the top of the leg after cutting. Note the use of masking tape as a guide line and 'chip-retainer'.

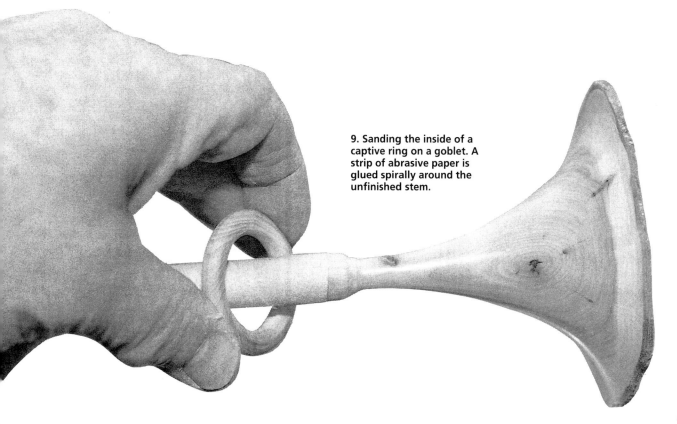

9. Sanding the inside of a captive ring on a goblet. A strip of abrasive paper is glued spirally around the unfinished stem.

10. Brass nipple bonded into place before turning of the lamp base commences. (Tailstock removed for clarity.)

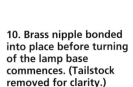

12. Backs of picture frames showing turn-buttons. The retaining screws occupy the holes for attaching the frames to dummy faceplates.

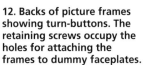

11. Finished lamp base before removal from the lathe. Note how the neck matches the lamp-holder. (Tailstock removed for clarity.)

from the shaft.

But there will always be a little ridge on the inside edge of each ring which cannot be removed with a cutting tool, and rubbing this away with abrasive paper is difficult in the confined space available.

Difficult, that is, unless you adopt my wheeze! Once the rings are all parted off, turn the shaft to a uniform diameter somewhat larger than its finished size. Now glue a spiral strip of abrasive paper around the shaft, pushing the rings to one end or the other as required.

With the lathe running, you can take each ring in turn, and wiggle it about until 'the parts which other devices can't reach' are nice and smooth (Photo 9). Then the abrasive paper is stripped off, and the shaft turned down to its final size.

So what's new about table lamp bases? Not a lot – you take a fair-sized block of wood, mount it between centres, and bore half-way into it with an 8mm (5⁄16in) auger passing through the hollow tailstock. Then you reverse it end-to-end, fit a four-pronged drive with an 8mm (5⁄16in) pilot into the headstock, and bore through again.

Next, you hold the workpiece firmly to allow the drive to bore a hole into the base, making a recess where the flex will turn through 90°. Finally, you turn the block to an attractive shape, and drill a transverse hole into the recess for the flex.

Finally, did I say? Not quite – there's a little wheeze that comes first. I like to turn the neck of a lamp base to a small diameter compatible with the size of the bottom of the lampholder, which I attach to the base via a brass nipple. If I start turning the base

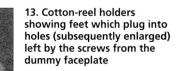

13. Cotton-reel holders showing feet which plug into holes (subsequently enlarged) left by the screws from the dummy faceplate

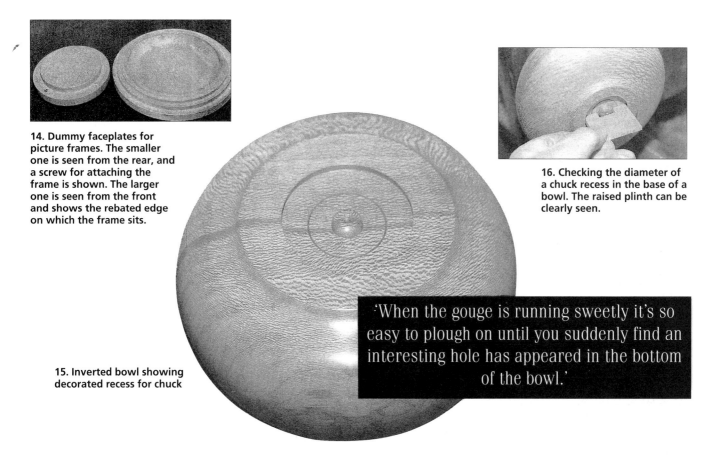

14. Dummy faceplates for picture frames. The smaller one is seen from the rear, and a screw for attaching the frame is shown. The larger one is seen from the front and shows the rebated edge on which the frame sits.

16. Checking the diameter of a chuck recess in the base of a bowl. The raised plinth can be clearly seen.

15. Inverted bowl showing decorated recess for chuck

'When the gouge is running sweetly it's so easy to plough on until you suddenly find an interesting hole has appeared in the bottom of the bowl.'

without taking some precautions, I am going to risk splitting the top end by the wedge action of the tail centre when the diameter is reduced.

The wheeze is to Araldite the nipple in place before the shaping commences (Photo 10). The nipple will react the wedge action without putting any lateral pressure on the wood, and the lampholder is guaranteed to be concentric with the base because the nipple is automatically on dead centre. Moreover, the adhesive will reduce the danger of splitting the neck, since the wood is firmly bonded to the brass nipple.

Note that you need a revolving tail centre – the friction between the nipple and a fixed centre would cause serious problems. From time to time it is advisable to withdraw the centre and screw on the lampholder in order to ensure an exact match (Photo 11).

Let's leave spindle-turning now, and look at faceplate and chuck work, where the old argument of screw-holes versus chuck recesses appears to be still going on. There are those who regard screw-holes, even when they are subsequently filled with plastic wood, as unsightly. Even worse than plastic wood, to some eyes, is a covering of green baize. My own view is that screw-holes should be eliminated if at all possible, but I accept that there will always be cases when they are unavoidable.

Do you remember the Father Brown story about a murder in broad daylight in a block of flats? All the eye-witnesses swore that no-one had entered or left the building during the critical time. Eventually it transpired that the murderer had been disguised as the postman, but nobody counted him as a visitor – he just seemed

to be doing his job.

It can be the same with screw-holes. People will turn over one of your *objets d'art*, and not see any screw-holes. But they will be there, just the same. How's it done? Well, one wheeze is to fill them with screws! Of course, the screws have to serve a useful purpose. One typical instance is to retain the little turn-buttons on the back of a picture-frame (Photo 12).

Another wheeze for disguising the holes is to drill them oversize after they have served their original purpose of fixing the workpiece to the faceplate, and then use them to locate tiny mushroom-shaped feet under the base of a teapot stand or a cotton-reel holder (Photo 13).

'But', I hear you saying, 'The pitch circle diameter of the screw-holes in my faceplate isn't the size I want.' Or 'The faceplate has four holes and I want to have only three feet on my teapot stand'. You need a widget – make a dummy faceplate!

A disc of scrap is drilled with two sets of holes. One set corresponds with the holes in the steel faceplate, and the other set is arranged to suit the job in hand. The dummy faceplate can even have a rebated edge which will locate a partly-turned picture-frame, for example (Photo 14).

Bowls

Every turner makes bowls, and there's not much I can add to the vast store of knowledge on the subject of bowl-turning. Like everyone else, I suppose, I start the job by screwing the workpiece

17. Anti-skid grooves in top of bowl. The screw-holes for the faceplate can still be seen, and hollowing-out has just commenced.

18. Simple depth-gauge in use

19. Depth gauge made from marking-out gauge

20. A part-finished pear-shaped box. Both halves have been hollowed out, and the base is being driven through the lid. Note the use of masking tape to ensure a positive drive. The stub at the tailstock end will be saved for later use.

21. The base of the pear-shaped box after being jammed on to a stub for finishing. Masking tape is used to reinforce the jam.

to the faceplate, or by mounting it on a pin chuck or a screw chuck, while I turn the outside.

Whatever the method of mounting, any signs of it will be eliminated when the inside is hollowed out, so there's no need to worry about that.

I favour the expanding chuck for the second phase. I know screws-through-faceplates and hot-melt-glue-to-dummy-faceplates have their proponents, mainly because they think the chuck recess is unsightly. But the recess can be made into a thing of beauty – there's no need for it to be just a flat uninteresting cavity.

The centre of the recess makes no contact with the expanding jaws so why not turn an attractive boss in the middle? (Did you know the boss in the centre of a shield is called an 'umbo'? There was that dreadful clue in the crossword – 'The boss is a headless elephant!')

Add some more decoration by cutting one or two rings around the umbo with the point of a skew, and then no-one (fellow turners excepted) will appreciate the true purpose of the recess (Photo 15).

One obvious widget at this stage is a gauge for the diameter and flatness of the recess. This is just a piece of thin scrap with a straight edge, and as wide as the required diameter. If you go for an umbo, you will need to cut away the edge locally to clear it (Photo 16).

Some turners feel that the presence of the recess necessitates an increase in wall thickness towards the bottom of the bowl. But if you turn a shallow plinth of the same height as the depth of the recess and a little greater in diameter, the wall thickness can be kept virtually constant. I feel a bowl looks better if it is raised up slightly on a plinth.

Once the bowl is mounted on the expanding chuck I adopt another wheeze before I start hollowing out. With the point of a skew, I cut a series of 'anti-skid' grooves across the flat surface of the rotating workpiece (Photo 17). These ensure that my bowl gouge won't suddenly shoot off sideways and chip the edge – or maybe that never happens to you!

Before we leave bowl-turning, let me mention a well-known widget – the depth gauge. When the gouge is running sweetly it's so easy to plough on until you suddenly find an interesting hole has appeared in the bottom of the bowl. If you have cut a ring around the umbo, the hole will correspond with the ring, and leave a nice clean edge. If you haven't cut a ring, you'll have a nasty jagged edge.

This isn't a reason for adopting my ring idea – any kind of hole is a nuisance, but the clean hole can be reclaimed more easily. Just turn a plug in a contrasting wood, and pretend you always meant the bowl to look like that!

But I have digressed again. All you need for a depth gauge is a strip of wood with a hole in it. Through this passes a dowel with a rounded end. If the hole is drilled slightly undersize, a saw cut down the length of the dowel will ensure a tight fit. Set the gauge by adjusting the dowel until the amount projecting is equal to the required internal depth of the bowl (Photo 18).

Apply the gauge at intervals until the crossbar just rests on the edge, then stop cutting. Clearly, it's best to set the gauge a fraction on the low side so you have some warning of an impending disaster.

If you want to make a gauge with a more positive clamping action, you can always slip the crossbar over the stem of a marking-out gauge (Photo 19). Clamping the block will prevent the crossbar from slipping to a depth greater than the one you intended. Either version of the gauge can, of course, be used in the reverse manner to measure the depth at any particular stage.

Boxes

I'm not going to describe how to make a box – like bowl-turning, enough has been written on that subject already. But I must mention this wheeze. Where you rely on friction so the lid can be turned by driving it via the base (or vice versa), a band of masking tape will ensure no slippage occurs (Photo 20). I always keep a roll of tape handy on the bench. It has many uses, such as acting as a depth gauge on a drill, or holding things together until the glue sets, or for wrapping round a peg to make it fit an oversize hole.

I usually finish the base (or the top) of a box by jamming it on to a spigot held in a chuck, so one further wheeze is to save the stubs from your box-turning. There's usually a stub left at the end, which is already adapted to fit in the chuck. It can easily be turned down to an exact fit next time you need to finish a box.

Here again the masking tape comes in useful to reinforce the 'jam' (Photo 21). Alternatively, the stub can become a spigot for turning a thimble, or have a hole drilled in it to make a home-made screw chuck.

Pencil-holders

I used to make a lot of pencil-holders, but the bottom seems to have dropped out of the market lately. If your customers are still buying them, and you are making them by the dozen, you may decide to make a jig to simplify drilling the pattern of holes in the top.

My holders are usually bun-shaped, so my jig is an inverted bowl which fits over the holder (Photo 22). It has a flat top which is covered with sheet brass to minimise the wear of the holes by the drill.

I start the holder on a screw-chuck so that I can cut a recess (with an umbo!) in the base. After drilling a pilot hole for the screw chuck, I open up the first 3mm (⅛in) of the hole so the threads do not engage in this short section. This wheeze ensures that the screw does not raise flakes of wood on the outer surface. These often spread outwards, and mar the finished job.

After finishing the base on the screw-chuck, the holder is reversed and mounted on an expanding chuck. The screw-chuck hole can now be opened up along its full length to make it big enough to take a pencil – another instance of an invisible screw-hole.

The holder is then turned to its final shape and removed from the lathe. It is placed on the table of the bench drill with the drill jig over it, located by a peg through the central hole. One of the

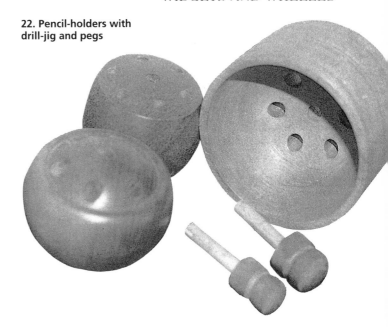

22. Pencil-holders with drill-jig and pegs

surrounding holes is then drilled, and a second peg inserted (Photo 23) to prevent any relative rotation, after which the remaining holes are drilled. I find a lip-and-spur bit gives the cleanest holes, especially on a sloping surface.

Stools

I was making some high four-legged stools recently. These are fascinating things to make, because every piece – seat, legs and stretchers – is turned. The seat is a straightforward piece of faceplate and chuck work – and yes, mine has screw-holes on the underside which are filled with plastic wood. I really should have

23. Pencil-holder being drilled through a jig. Note the two locating pegs and the brass face on the jig.

24. Drill-jig for seat and legs of stools. The base-board with its hinged flap is resting on the bed bars, while the carriers for the seat and the legs are standing against the window. A dummy stretcher and the angle-gauge are in the foreground.

made a dummy faceplate with screws which would have coincided with the holes for the legs.

The legs and stretchers are equally simple pieces of spindle turning. The tricky bits are drilling the holes in the seat for the legs, and the holes in the legs for the stretchers.

First of all, you must decide on an angle (α) for the splay of the legs. The legs have an exposed length of *l* (there is a short length of spigot buried in the seat) and the seat is drilled with four holes on a pitch circle of radius *r*. The feet rest on a circle of radius *R*. This means that

$$sin\ \alpha = (R - r) \div l$$
In my case, $l = 20in$,
$R = 8in$ and $r = 4.5in$,
giving $sin\ \alpha = 0.175$
whence $\alpha = 20°$ approx.

Another calculation shows that ß, the complement of the angle between the stretchers and the legs, is given by

$$sin\ \beta = sin\ \alpha \div \sqrt{2}$$
i.e. $sin\ \beta = 0.707\ sin\ \alpha$
For my stools, $\beta = 7°$ approx.

On previous occasions I had drilled the seat and the legs on my bench drill, making use of the tilting table to give me the angles I needed. I hit two snags: (1) the size of the seat meant its edge fouled the pillar of the drill, so the seat had to be slewed round to get the hole centre under the drill point, resulting in a slightly compound angle; (2) the shape of a leg made it a very wobby fit in the V-block I used to support it.

For the latest set of tools, I resolved to make a jig which would enable both seats and legs to be drilled on the lathe. The jig was to be adjustable so seats of various sizes, and legs of different lengths and diameters, could be drilled at any likely angle.

The resulting widget (Photo 24) has a base-board which slides along the bed bars, guided by a wooden block which is a good fit between them. The drill is mounted in a chuck in the headstock, and the jig is pushed towards the drill by advancing the tailstock against a vertical back-board.

25. Stool seat ready for drilling in the jig

26. Stool leg (inverted) in the drill-jig. One hole has been drilled, and now carries the dummy stretcher to enable the leg to be rotated to the correct orientation for the second hole.

27. Leg-trimmer in use. The cradle carrying the leg is clamped to the mitre fence of the band saw. Note the use of a dummy stretcher and triangular sighting board to ensure correct orientation of the leg.

Incidentally, I have modified the tailstock of my Coronet so it has a bigger wheel (an elm disc) with a handle. It makes horizontal boring much easier, and the tailstock can be wound in and out much quicker. Record Power, please note!

The leading edge of the base-board carries a hinged flap of 12mm (½in) plywood, which is fixed at the required angle to the vertical by means of a slotted stay sliding on a bolt equipped with a wing-nut. The stay came from the local DIY store – it was sold for use on a writing desk flap.

A hollow board made from two sheets of plywood separated by narrow edge pieces slips over the hinged flap. The rear face is slotted to pass over a bolt whose head is recessed into the flap. Another wing-nut and a large washer on this bolt serve to clamp the board at any desired height. The front face of the board carries two strips of wood to make a V-block.

The seat is placed in the V-block (Photo 25) and the hinged flap is inclined at the correct angle (a), using a triangular template as a gauge. (There's no need to measure the angle with a protractor. Since you know the sine of the angle, it's a simple matter to draw a right-angled triangle with its shortest side and its hypotenuse in the correct ratio.)

The V-block is then raised or lowered until the drill point is on the pitch circle for the leg holes. This circle can be scribed or drawn before the seat is removed from the lathe.

The tailstock is then wound forward, propelling the jig towards the rotating drill, and a clean hole at the correct angle is guaranteed every time. A saw-tooth or Forstner bit is recommended – but make sure you know when to stop drilling! You can quite easily put a limit on the depth of the hole by arranging for the tailstock screw to hit the end of its travel before you go too deep.

A second board is made to fit over the hinged flap to carry the leg. In this case, the V-block is replaced by an extension which fits between the bed bars. Two brackets – one at the top of the board, and one at the bottom of this extension – support the leg, which is mounted upside-down.

The upper bracket can slide up and down the board to accommodate legs of various lengths, and carries an adjustable pointed screw which clamps the leg in position by engaging the hole previously occupied by the tail centre. The lower bracket has a hole of the same diameter as those which have just been drilled in the seat, and into this fits the spigot on the leg.

This bracket should be replaceable, so that spigots of different diameters can be accepted. It is important to make sure the centre-line of the leg is parallel to the board and that it intercepts the axis of the lathe.

The drilling procedure is exactly as described for the seat, first setting the angle ß, then adjusting the height of the leg to ensure that the drill hits it at the correct spot, and finally extending the tailstock to push the workpiece towards the drill.

Once one hole has been drilled, the leg must be raised or lowered so it can be positioned for the second hole. The question then arises: 'How far do I twist it round?' My solution is to use a dummy stretcher, consisting of a short length of rectangular section with a spigot at one end which is a good fit in the first hole.

The leg is rotated until a try-square, with its edge held against the dummy stretcher, has its blade parallel to the axis of the drill (Photo 26). The leg is then in the correct position for drilling, but be sure to rotate the leg in the right direction – two go one way, and two go the other.

I developed three more widgets and a wheeze to help in the final stages of stool-making. The first is the leg-trimmer. Up to this stage, the legs have been left with square-cut ends, but they need to be trimmed off at an angle so they sit firmly on the floor. They also need to be all exactly the same length.

Now the reference point for all the work on the legs is a small shoulder abutting against the underside of the seat, which is obviously at a fixed height above the floor. The leg-drilling jig and the leg-trimmer therefore rely on this shoulder to locate the leg before operating on it.

The leg-trimmer is simply a cradle rather like the leg-drilling jig, except the lower portion of the leg is supported in a bracket which can be slid along the tapering leg until it fits snugly. The cradle is clamped firmly to the mitre fence of the band saw so the shoulder is positioned at the predetermined distance from the band saw blade.

The fence is inclined at the same angle (α) as the seat on the seat-drilling jig, using the same setting-gauge. This widget will ensure every leg is cut off at the same angle and the same length.

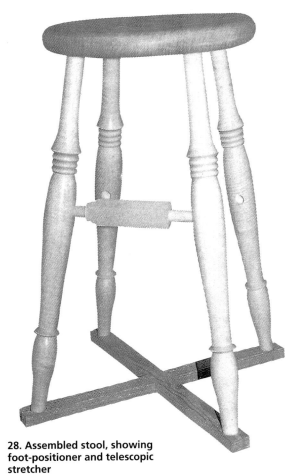

28. Assembled stool, showing foot-positioner and telescopic stretcher

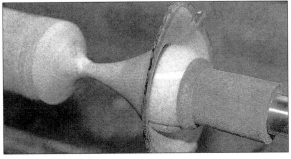

29. Tennis-ball widget in use, supporting the cup of a goblet while the stem is turned

The wheeze is to ensure the leg is rotated to the right orientation before the end is trimmed. This is achieved by inserting the dummy stretcher into one of the sockets, and making sure it is inclined at 45° to the surface of the saw table (Photo 27).

My next widget is the foot-positioner. This is simply a cross made from two strips of wood with a half-lap joint at the centre. Recesses, slightly larger than the diameter of the feet, are drilled at the end of each arm so when the stool stands on the cross with the feet in the recesses, the feet are on the correct pitch circle.

This widget has two uses: first for the temporary positioning of the legs while determining the length of the stretchers (Photo 28), and second for ensuring correct positioning during final assembly.

The last widget is the telescopic stretcher. This is a short length of square-section wood bored part-way through to the same diameter as the holes in the legs, and with a spigot turned on the other end.

A short length of dowel is a sliding fit inside the hole, making a telescopic device which can be expanded into position as a dummy stretcher (Photo 28). A pencil line can then be drawn on the dowel to enable the expanded length to be measured after the widget has been removed.

And finally, I've just thought up another widget which really belongs under 'between centres'. I was turning a tall goblet with a trumpet-shaped cup, and needed something to support the cup while I turned the slender stem.

I hit on the idea of using a tennis ball – it has a fluffy surface, so it doesn't scratch the inside of the cup, and it's spherical, so it fits inside almost any hollow shape with a circular cross-section.

The ball is glued into a shallow recess on the end of a hollow wooden cylinder which slips over the revolving centre (Photo 29). I've since used it on several occasions, for goblets of various sizes, and found it most effective. I bought my tennis ball from a toyshop for 75p, and the widget was made in 10 minutes.

So those are all my widgets and wheezes – or at least, all that haven't already been published.

This article originally appeared in two parts in *Woodturning* issues 10 and 11, Sept/Oct 1992 and Nov/Dec 1992.

Details of Coronet Lathes from Record Power Ltd.

Basic metalwork for woodturners

Metalwork and basic engineering skills can come in very handy for the woodturner. Mike describes some simple modifications to make life easier on the lathe.

Mike Foden

There is no doubt that a basic knowledge of engineering can be a great asset to the woodturner. But if anyone had suggested a few years ago that I might attempt metalwork, I would have forcibly rejected the idea.

Wood is a living, warm material full of surprises in grain, colour and density. While working with wood there is always a new world to be discovered, as no two pieces are alike. Metal, on the other hand, is cold, hard and heavy. It is unyielding and has a predetermined density – no surprises here. However, after some five years of metalwork I feel fully confident in this medium and it now makes a pleasant diversion from woodturning.

I would urge all woodturners to 'have a go', and if possible obtain a metalworking lathe. Second-hand machines can be had for reasonable prices due to many engineering firms closing because of the recession. Do not despair, though, if you have not got a metal working lathe, as much interesting work can be achieved with hand tools alone and by adapting your woodturning lathe.

Once again many accessories can be obtained from firms closing down, and by diligent searching through magazines and adverts in the local paper. I have obtained dozens of HSS taps and dies very cheaply which would normally retail for a substantial sum (Photo 2).

My five-speed bench drill, costing less than £80 new, has proved indispensable. It is solid, accurate and reliable (Photo 3). How I managed both woodwork and metalwork for years without one, I will never know.

The addition of two sturdy cross slides/vices has extended the possibilities, especially for metalwork. The cross slides sell for only £20, and when you consider that the whole set-up cost less than some industrial hand-held electric drills (or even a drill stand by some manufacturers) it makes you stop and wonder how you should be spending your hard-earned cash.

With a set of taps and dies you can cut internal and external threads in metal and some of the harder woods. To ensure the tap starts cutting squarely use it in the bench drill, turning it by hand, and then complete the threading freehand with a tap wrench, or start the cut by placing the tap in a drill chuck in the tailstock.

A simple die stock holder is either purchased or made to be used in the lathe tailstock barrel, making sure that it has the correct morse taper for your machine (Photo 4).

All you need to ensure is that the workpiece is prepared to the right diameter for external threads, or drilled to the right size for internal threads. Charts containing the relevant information are available at negligible cost.

1. Selection of holders and wrenches

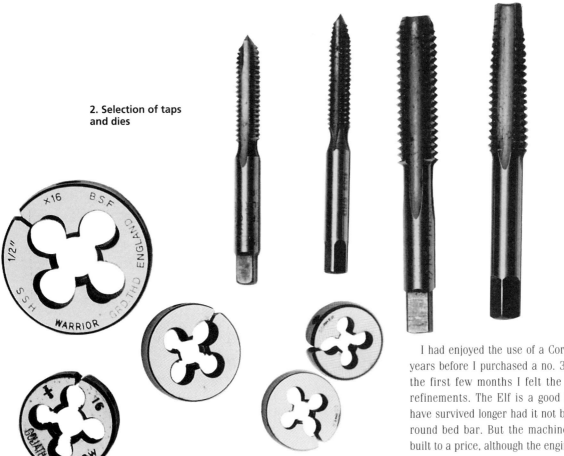

2. Selection of taps and dies

Much of my metalwork is in brass, and this can be obtained cheaply from a scrap metal yard who will outsort brass from other metals. Avoid buying new material, as it can prove expensive.

Brass is easily worked by hand with HSS cutting tools or scrapers and an excellent finish is possible straight from the tool. If abrasives are required, use emery cloth with oil and finish with T-cut abrasive polish.

It is useful to have a means of dividing on the lathe and, although division plates are available, the turner will need to make a detent himself (Photo 5).

Do not be frightened to drill and tap a thread in the headstock. I have drilled my Myford and my Coronet no. 3 lathe in several places to accommodate various fitments and improvements. All the work was completed freehand with a hand-held drill and taps, and has proved eminently successful.

As an example of savings it should be noted that a threaded Morse taper adaptor to hold a drill chuck in the tailstock will cost you about £23. With screw cutting facilities it is possible to buy a Morse taper blank for £3 and thread your own in a few minutes, thereby creating a substantial saving.

3. My trusty 5-speed bench drill

I had enjoyed the use of a Coronet Elf for many years before I purchased a no. 3 lathe, but within the first few months I felt the need for certain refinements. The Elf is a good lathe, and would have survived longer had it not been for the single round bed bar. But the machine was, of course, built to a price, although the engineering was good.

The no. 3 lathe incorporates some of the best features of the Elf, has a double bar bed, is heavier and has a more substantial spindle and bearing.

My first job was to put handles on the tailstock wheel (Photo 6). I had become accustomed to this facility on the Elf, and there is no way a tailstock can be operated smoothly without handles. It is particularly useful in drilling operations, and very easy to hand turn one from 10mm (⅜in) brass bar.

Put a clearance hole through the handwheel in one or two places and drill and tap the brass handle. A matching screw secures the handle to the wheel. This method is easier as it involves threading the brass instead of the cast iron wheel.

At the other end of the lathe, I found that to lock the spindle for removal of chucks etc. a heavy cast plate had to be removed, and then an ill-fitting spanner had to be located on the spindle at a very awkward angle. I felt it would have been a simple matter to have left an extra 25mm (1in) on the spindle at the manufacturing stage with spanner flats or a tommy bar hole. The makers advised me that this would have been a safety hazard, but I disagree.

Some of the world's finest woodturning lathes incorporate a good sized handwheel at the outboard end of the spindle, and many desirable machines have an extra threaded section protruding for outboard turning.

4. Home-made tailstock die holder

5. Division plate and detent

6. Brass handles fitted to the tailstock wheel on my no. 3

I discovered a way around the problem was to drill and tap the spindle. This is done freehand again, and is most easily accomplished by swivelling the headstock anti-clockwise. Persistence is needed as the spindle is hardened, and take great care when tapping as the taps can easily break off in the hard material.

The brass handwheel can be trued up while on the lathe by swivelling the headstock and bringing round the tool rest. A small handle is added similar to that on the tailstock (Photo 7) and holes drilled for a tommy bar to lock the spindle.

With a wheel, it is now easier to screw the chuck or faceplate onto the spindle especially with a heavy workpiece, as the handwheel does all the work while the chuck and workpiece are held stationary.

Handwheel

My main complaint with the Elf was that you needed a spanner to move the tool rest. That is no longer true with the no. 3 but a handwheel is lacking on the spindle end.

The heavy four-jaw chuck is popular with woodturners, but it is a two-handed job to remove or replace it on the spindle and, of course, the spindle has to be locked with the spanner.

An amateur woodturner will frequently change chucks, and a handwheel makes life a lot easier, especially when unscrewing, as all that is required is one hand to support the weight and one to turn the wheel. It is almost impossible to drop the chuck on the bed bars using this method.

The Coronet no. 3 is intended for bench mounting, and although the motor is quiet enough, and the lathe runs smoothly, it will be found that when the machine is bolted onto a hardwood bench top, the vibration and sound can be a little overpowering.

Being a great believer in quiet machinery, be it my car or my lathe, I decided something had to be done. A softwood bench top would absorb sound more easily than my 45mm (1¾in) thick beech top, so I tried padding with rubber mats. This did little to improve matters, as the hardwood top acted like an amplifier, even though it was bolted to the concrete floor and the brick walls.

After much experimenting I discovered that by releasing the belt tension a little, the sound was reduced dramatically. Having selected the speed, I lifted the motor slightly and tightened the motor clamping bolt. This system is more effective at the higher speeds, and the tool may arrest the work if a heavy cut is taken at the lower speeds. However, if the tools are sharpened properly all should be well, and an incorrect cut will tend to stop the work rotating instead of producing a dig in. This can only be beneficial to the turner.

My next refinement was to hinge the heavy cast pulley cover plate, which is more convenient than having to remove it completely to change speed.

Finally I will tell you about a problem I encountered and how to avoid it. Having placed a four-jaw chuck on the spindle I proceeded to turn a small item. After a couple of minutes I stopped the lathe to examine the work. When I restarted, I saw the four-jaw jump backwards towards the bearings. Somehow it had loosened slightly and unscrewed itself a fraction when the lathe stopped. Starting up again locked the chuck solidly onto the spindle.

I am no stranger to jammed lathe chucks and indeed I have used every trick over the years with success. In theory I should have been able to lock the spindle with the spanner provided and, after placing the key in one of the chuck recesses, give it a sharp tap with a hammer to release it.

Alas, it was not so simple, and after some time the spanner became distorted and useless. I flooded the spindle nose with lubricants and left it overnight, but the following morning showed no improvement. Tommy bars used in the handwheel became twisted. I removed the chuck jaws and put a long length of steel bar across the jaw ways, but this also proved unsuccessful.

Eventually I realised that the spindle had to be kept absolutely still while the chuck was removed. I got a substantial adjustable spanner which, when fully opened, was not quite wide enough to fit the spindle flats. I ground it out to tightly fit the flats and fixed it in position against the headstock casting.

A normal open-ended spanner of the correct size for the flats was much too loose. I removed the cross bar from the chuck key and put a length of tube over the key. Quite suddenly it was all over – a total of some four hours hard labour, and a lot of worry.

7. Brass handwheel and handle fitted to the outboard end of the spindle

Moral

There is a moral to this story. Always place a fine brass or copper washer on the spindle before screwing on a chuck. Washers only 1mm thick are available from car accessory shops (Photo 8).

Alternatively, always use a tommy bar to nip up the chuck slightly before turning so it cannot come loose and then over-tighten when the lathe is restarted. In theory, it should be self-tightening in use, but theory has never been an exact science!

I hope these ideas may prove of some use and you will be encouraged to attempt a little metal work of your own. Believe me, it is very satisfying to make something yourself that will enhance your lathe and make your turning a little easier.

This article originally appeared in *Woodturning* issue 12, Jan/Feb 1993.

Details of Coronet Lathes from Record Power Ltd.

8. Always fit a thin brass or copper washer on the spindle before screwing on a chuck.

'Believe me, it is very satisfying to make something yourself that will enhance your lathe and make your turning a little easier.'

Papering the cracks

Old methods are often the best, says Ernie, as he takes a fresh look at using paper joints in turning.

Ernie Conover

With the current fascination with metal chucks, and new ones coming out every day, turners are often ignorant of how good many of the old tried and true methods are.

Traditional methods will often do the job better and cheaper than so-called modern methods. Such a case can be made for the paper joint.

In talking to a good many turners as I travel around doing workshops, I realise most are aware of the paper joint, but have never tried it. Let us demystify the paper joint so we can add it to our bag of turning tricks.

Most are familiar with the use of the paper joint in making split turnings. Both in architecture and furniture construction, quartered or halved turnings are often applied to exposed faces. While such turnings sometimes buttress an overhang, they are mostly for decorative purposes.

I first became familiar with the benefits of the paper joint in producing just such turnings. They were not for furniture, however, but rather for pattern making. Wood patterns are what a foundry uses to make impressions in sand for casting metal.

Since my casting was mostly around the Conover lathe my patterns were for cast iron. Even today, paper joints are one of the most powerful weapons in the pattern maker's arsenal.

Since many castings are round, turning is a large part of the pattern maker's art. A pattern is made by halves and the two halves are mounted on opposite sides of a board, called a match plate, but in perfect alignment with each other.

Sawing a finished turning in two, even with the thinnest of saws, removes enough material that one is left with an incomplete circle. The subsequent part cast from such a pattern will be decidedly oval.

Paper joints overcome this problem by creating a hairline split in the finished part. Some care must be taken to centre perfectly on the paper joint during turning.

The piece turns normally and you cannot tell any difference from

a normal billet. Once turned, however, the work magically separates into two perfect hemispheres when a sharp chisel is inserted in the joint and nudged with a mallet.

The basis of a working paper joint is brown craft paper and some hide glue – what is called Scotch glue in the UK. Polyvinyl acetate (PVA) cold glues will also work acceptably in a paper joint, but not,

1. Craft paper

in my experience, as well as hide glue.

It must, however, be real hide glue that is cooked in a glue pot, not the modern liquid stuff that is sold in small bottles. Liquid hide glue is next to worthless, because to make it liquid at room temperature, large amounts of acetic acid are added and this sacrifices much of the glue's strength. No, we want the real thing, the kind you boil in a pot.

If you do not have a glue pot, fear not: you can still improvise something suitable. You need to warm the glue but not boil the mixture – it should never exceed 54° C (129.2° F).

Most old books recommend a pot with a water jacket around it, but most modern pots work dry. Therefore, a double boiler on a hot plate set to an appropriate low temperature works fine. Also baby bottle warmers abound at garage sales and are perfect.

I think hide glue is superior for all my joinery, so feel that a pot is well worth the investment. Scotch glue is easily repairable if the joint fails; the excess wipes off easily, but if left on the exposed surfaces it does not affect the finish (polish).

Hide glue is sold in pellet form. To make up a batch mix equal weights of water and glue. While a scale is useful, I have never had the luxury of one. I just put a handful of pellets in the pot and cover them with water.

Stir the mixture as it heats and the pellets dissolve. You want a viscous mixture, about the consistency of honey. If the mixture is too thin, add pellets or let the pot simmer for a while. If it is too thick add water and stir. Nothing could be simpler.

Now the glue is heating you need to find some brown craft paper. In the USA groceries are packed in bags of the perfect weight material (Photo 1). In the UK packages are often wrapped for mailing in such paper. What you want is a heavy strong paper.

To make a split turning you need two sections of timber that are half the desired billet. In the case of a quartered turning you need four. There should be a joinery level fit between the glued surfaces. I hand plane until I have a perfect fit (Photo 2), but a power jointer works well if the pieces are large enough. Never power joint anything shorter than about 200mm (8in).

Rub both halves of the workpiece with Scotch glue (Photos 3 and 4) and press them together with the paper in between. If the workshop is cold, it is best to warm the pieces a bit. I do this with a hair dryer.

Once perfectly juxtaposed, clamp with moderate pressure. I usually trim the excess paper at this time with a sharp knife (Photo 5). You need to leave the clamps in place for at least 12 hours (Photo 6).

The drying process for hide glue is in two stages. First it jells, which happens the second it drops in temperature, then the water is absorbed and/or evaporates, which takes the 12 plus hours.

If within the first hour or so you decide alignment is wrong, some heat from a hair dryer will allow repositioning. Even once dry the glue can be softened by streaming with a kettle or soaking with hot water.

I mix only small amounts, because hide glue has a definite pot life. It should be clear and honey-like. If it smells rancid, it is.

When my two Labrador retrievers start worshipping the glue pot I know it is time to make a fresh batch. They love to chew on any glue-laden scraps and it won't hurt them a bit.

Once dry, chuck the workpiece perfectly on centre and turn normally. I usually try to use a cup tailstock centre, rather than a 60° point so as not to split the joint. I also align the tines or prongs of my drive centre so that no tine is on the joint.

Once the piece is turned and finished (polished), place a wide, sharp chisel in the joint and tap with a mallet (Photo 7). Hey presto – the piece will drop into two perfect halves (Photo 8).

It is possible to make split faceplate turnings equally well with paper joints. Again, for pattern makers this is common practice. You do want to split faceplate turnings along the plank grain and **do not glue exposed end grain.** Glue will have no strength on end grain so gluing the plank grain avoids a glue failure.

Chucking

Another use of paper joints is chucking. Most turners are vaguely familiar with paper joint chucking, but it is my hunch that few have

2. Hand planing the blank for a perfect fit

3. Applying the glue to the backing block

4. More hide glue

5. Trimming paper to size of glue block

ever tried it. Instead, I find that most turners have fiddled with the modern substitute for the paper joint – double-sided tape.

I will admit we cling to the methods we were first taught, but I have tried double-sided tape and think it does not work as well as the time-honoured paper joint. While a paper joint lets loose when I decide it is time, double-sided tape can be a problem to separate. I have had to pull wood away from the turning, causing much extra work. The paper joint will separate perfectly and hide glue can be washed off with warm water or scraped away with a cabinet scraper.

Many turners have told me they have had the same separation problem with paper joints. When I scrutinise, invariably they have used one or another of the cold glues. Cold glues have a tendency to soak through the craft paper, forming a permanent bond. Hide glue will never give this problem.

Paper joint chucking is perfect for thin faceplate turnings such as plates, trays, escutcheons, and medallions (Photo 9). Safety wise the main thing is to keep the area of the paper joint proportional to the size of the turning.

You cannot chuck a 405mm (16in) diameter plate on a 75mm (3in) diameter paper joint. You need at least a 150mm (6in) diameter joint (Fig 1). The important thing is the area of the joint, which should be at least 15 per cent of the area of one side of the blank.

The above-mentioned turnings are done from dry timber and accurately bandsawn to rough size before mounting in the lathe so there is a balanced load to start with.

6. Clamp for a minimum of 12 hours and preferably 24 hours

First cuts should be at a slow speed of 600 rpm or so. Once trued up, speed can be increased but should never exceed 1,100 rpm.

As with our spindle turnings, both the turning and the glue block should be planed for a perfect glue joint. Good joinery practice says to align the grains of the two pieces and not cross them. I think this would be of little consequence, however, since there is paper between them and the piece will be turned soon. Still, good workshop practice never killed anyone!

In closing, I hope you give paper joints a whirl. They solve some problems and are a cheap and effective chuck. Try it and you will see that what I am telling you is not a tissue of lies.

This article originally appeared in *Woodturning* issue 13, March/April 1993.

7. After turning place a large chisel on the plank grain side of the joint and tap with a mallet.

8. The parted joint

Workpiece

Wood glue block

Faceplate

Brown craft paper

75mm (3in)
150mm (6in)
405mm (16in)

Fig 1 Typical paper joint chucking

9. The finished tray

Sandblasting

Bowl etching using sandblasting techniques

Albert Clarke

For the last 15 years I have taken part in craft fairs and gallery shows along the Pacific coast. I have had fun, made some cash, and lots of friends among the art and craft community.

The pieces that have attracted the most attention are lathe-turned items that have had a design etched on them by sandblasting.

Many of my designs have been strongly influenced by the beautiful ceramic pots of the South West American Indians, but you can use any inspiration. I find grape designs go well in California's wine country, and seagulls and fish sandblasted into redwood in coastal and harbour areas.

Before discussing the sandblasting process I will describe some modifications I made to my inexpensive lathe so it could cope with large blanks – I have found the public prefer large turnings to small ones.

First I extended the lathe base beyond the original bed so I could stand a tool steady/rest on the wood base instead of on the bed ways, or bars. I have never felt totally in control with a floor-standing toolrest when doing outboard turning. The base was made from building/construction timber boards 100mm x 150mm (4in x 6in) bolted and glued together to form a solid, rigid structure. This may sound like overkill, but the weight eliminates a good deal of vibration.

The tool rest stands on a 3mm (⅛in) steel plate which is bolted to the base with 12mm (½in) bolts and nuts. The tool rest is also heavy, being welded together from pieces of junkyard steel.

I also wanted to slow the lathe speed down for turning large items. I didn't want large pieces flying off because they were out of balance and turning too fast. Even if a blank is perfectly round it can still be out of balance because of different densities and

1. The design is laid out on the lathe.

2. Removing the stencil tape

3. Close-up of tape removal

uneven moisture content.

To slow the speed I put a 215mm (8½in) diameter mahogany disc onto the spindle by drilling a snug fitting hole to match the lathe. I married it to the existing pulley assembly by drilling and tapping into the metal pulley.

When the wood disc was securely fastened I cut a V-groove in it to match the V-drive belt. This groove was cut on the lathe in the

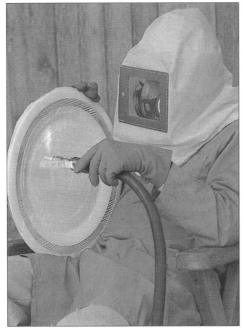

4. Kitted out in protective gear

5. The pressure blasting equipment

7. The perforations show clearly with the tape removed

6. Checking the perforations on a Douglas fir platter

normal way.

On my lathe, an old Rockwell, I had to cut away part of the cast iron pulley guard to make room for the larger wood pulley. I made a new guard from transparent acrylic sheet, leaving enough space to slip a V-belt past the large pulley to return the lathe to higher speeds when required.

The technique of sandblasting for decoration is similar to that used by signmakers to etch designs, but with a few twists. You will need masking material, a sharp knife or razor blade, protective clothing, a compressor and gun, and of course, sand.

Once you have finished turning your item, apply several coats of your favourite finishing material and allow to dry thoroughly. I use Varathane for natural finished woods, and car lacquers for items like *Wings* and *Side Winder*.

To prevent disasters on pitchy resinous woods like pine, redwood and fir I usually apply at least two coats of clear shellac to seal the wood, otherwise the finish may not set up in some areas.

It is helpful to leave the faceplate on the piece as it is easier to mark out patterns with the item on the lathe.

The essence of sandblasting is that you cover your turned item with masking tape and then cut out the pattern you want to blast.

There are several types of masking materials available for sandblasting, but I prefer polyvinyl chloride (PVC) tape with a release paper backing. I use Hartco Sandmask tape which comes in 9 metre (10 yard) rolls of 380mm (15in) and 635mm (25in) widths which costs $45 a roll including delivery.

Hartco recommend you don't stretch the material, but I find it will lay over a convex surface, such as a bowl, which requires a bit of stretching.

I try to avoid overlapping the material in areas which will

8. *The Fruit Basket*, pierced Douglas fir oval bowl, 420mm x 330mm x 75mm (16.5in x 13in x 3in)

receive the full blast of the sand. I use the old wallpaper-hanging trick of overlapping the joints and then cutting through both ends and removing the surplus.

This results in a perfect butt joint, but you must use a thin plastic protective backing piece underneath to prevent scoring the wood. It is OK to overlap the masking in areas not receiving the full force of the blast.

Before trying the masking material or blasting on a finished item I strongly recommend you try out the technique on a piece of scrap wood to get the feel of handling it.

When drawing the design on to the masking, it helps to clamp a block of wood to the tool rest (Photo 1). This makes it easier to draw radial lines on the workpiece. By holding a pencil on the block and tool rest while turning the bowl slowly by hand you can draw a perfect circle.

It is best to turn the wood by hand in case there is any slight warpage, in which case the pencil mark would not register completely round the circle if turning fast.

A dividing head can be helpful for marking out a geometric pattern, but I find dividers work just fine.

The masking tape cuts like Swiss cheese. You can use a sharp knife, but I prefer a razor blade – a throwback to my youth and passion for making model aeroplanes from balsa wood.

After cutting out your pattern stencil, you remove the tape from the areas to be sandblasted (Photos 2 and 3). In this case the bowl was sprayed black before masking.

Now for the sandblasting, and before you start make sure you are well covered with protective hood, mask, gown and gloves (Photo 4). The most important thing is to protect your face and lungs – the rest is to keep the sand out of your clothes and hair. I also wear rubber boots to prevent treading sand into the house.

At one time I used a sandblasting cabinet made from plywood and plastic sheeting. This meant I could save the sand, but it was rather cumbersome

9. Etched walnut bowl, 380mm x 125mm (15in x 5in)

10. *Gift from the Sea*, etched redwood bowl 380mm x 150mm (15in x 6in)

and impaired my visibility. As sand costs me only $4 for 100lbs and I use only a fraction of that to do a bowl, I no longer bother saving the sand but exhaust it out into the air.

You will need a good powerful compressor – there are lots to choose from. I started with a 1 hp model from Sears Roebuck which had enough pressure – 100 psi – but not enough flow in cubic feet per minute (cfm). It took too long to do a bowl because I had to keep waiting for the pressure to build up. I now use a 5 hp model with 110 psi and get about 8½ cfm. It cost about $450.

I tried siphon-type guns but now use a pressure pot system made by Waterloo Enterprises (Photo 5). This delivers a lot of sand in a short time, so you have to keep the gun moving at a steady rate. It takes only about 10 minutes to etch the pattern on a bowl.

One day I experimented with prolonging the sanding process to etch away the early, soft wood totally and leave the hard or late wood. This leaves a perforated, lattice-type effect (Photos 6, 7 and 8).

I find the best woods to use for this are redwood, fir, spruce and cedar because of their alternating hard and soft grain. It may make the bowl or platter look rather delicate, but the strength of the wood is mostly in the hard grain. I use 60 grit sand for this process, but you can use 30 grit.

If you are just etching a

pattern you can use hardwoods such as walnut (Photo 9). I also enjoy using local 'found' wood such as driftwood which I pick up along Tomales Bay near my home. I used such a piece of redwood for *Gift from the Sea* (Photo 10).

When you have finished the blasting, don't be in too much hurry to remove the rest of the tape. First give the blasted area at least two coats of shellac to seal it off. This prevents bleeding under the tape if you are going to use a pigmented material.

In Photos 9, 10 and 11, the sandblasted area was shot with a light coat of black lacquer and the highlights were hand-sanded to emphasise the texture of the grain. In Photos 12 and 13 a light blue-grey primer was sprayed on.

Now the big moment has arrived and you can carefully remove the rest of the tape. You have a spectacular piece for your next show, or at least to impress your friends.

This article originally appeared in *Woodturning* issue 13, March/April 1993.

11. *Stalactite*, etched redwood burl bowl 305mm x 230mm (12in x 9in)

12. *Wings*, lacquered and etched redwood bowl, 380mm x 125mm (15in x 5in)

13. *Side Winder*, lacquered and etched redwood bowl, 267mm x 160mm (10.5in x 6.25in)

Get hooked on rings

An expert in the use of hook and ring tools shares his knowledge of these very old inventions, which are now being rediscovered.

Kurt Johansson

I n 1968 one of my friends asked if I could turn a bowl from a block of glued up end grain pieces of pine. I very soon discovered that the tear-out was terrible when I tried to hollow out the bowl by using a round nose scraper. I then got the idea to use an old tool I had been using for hand-hollowing out bowls and kasas (two-handed Swedish drinking vessels) from birch-burls in the Lappish tradition (Photo 1).

After a number of tests I found the tool worked all right, the cuts were smooth and there was no tear-out. But the tool was too short and the shavings had a tendency to get stuck in the ring. So I went to my neighbour, the blacksmith, and made myself a hook-tool (Photo 2).

This tool worked quite well but was a bit unbalanced because the cutting did not take place in line with the tool shank. So back to the blacksmith's for some more forging. I made a few more hooks and finally ended up with one similar to the one in Photo 3. This one worked very well and I used it for several years.

The hook in Photo 3 is made by C.I. Fall in Sweden in HSS and can be bought from them or from Essve (UK) Ltd in England.

When I began to study old books on woodturning I found of course that the hook-tool was a very old invention. Several different hook-tools can be found in books like *Drechkunst* by J.M. Teuber from 1756, *Hand or Simple Turning* by Holtzapffel, *Das Drechselwerk* by Spannagel, or *Drechsein in Holtz* by Steinert.

Museum

The Swedish museum at Skokloster, not far from Stockholm, has one of the world's largest collections of woodturning tools from the seventeenth century. In this collection there are quite a lot of different hook-tools and other turning tools as well as several lathes.

The museum is strongly recommended to woodturners. When you visit Sweden and Stockholm, please get in touch with Mr Bengt Kylsberg who is in charge of the woodturning part of the museum.

When working with the hook-tools I experimented with different shapes and sizes but soon found that big hooks with an inner diameter of around 50mm (2in), while very good for finishing cuts in softwood, did not work well when used in hardwood or for rough turning. This was mainly because of excessive vibration.

After some time I discovered that if I made the inner diameter of the hook more or less the same as the diameter of the shank, the tool then seemed to be sturdy enough.

Many woodturners and blacksmiths have tried to make hook-tools. Too often they have copied old hook-tools from museums without realising that the tool they copied was a well used, sometimes completely worn-out tool.

In the book *Treen and Other Wooden Bygones* by E. Pinto there is a plate which shows a bottle turned in one piece and hollowed out through the neck. I thought if somebody had been able to do that before it should be possible to do it again. So I made up a set of bent hooks (Photo 4) and tried them out.

They worked very well, so I tried an even more angled version (Photo 5). With the angled tools it is very easy to turn bottles in end grain or other vessels with undercut rims.

The hook on the tool in Photo 5 is relatively small in comparison with the shank. If the hook is bigger, the tool will be rather difficult

1. Old ring-tool

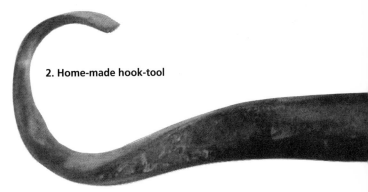

2. Home-made hook-tool

to control due to the long overhang of the cutting part.

See the book John Sainsbury's *Guide to Woodturning Tools and Equipment* for details on how to turn a bottle.

The hook-tool as such has its limitations. For example a hook-tool with an internal bevel does not work very well when hollowing out smaller objects such as egg-cups.

The bevel will not be rubbing, but the tool will be touching the working surface with the very tip of the cutting edge and the heel, which gives the tool a tendency to dig in or at least to cut very aggressively (Fig 1).

On the other hand a hook-tool with an external bevel (Fig 2) will not be able to work inside a smaller hollow because the cutting edge will not be able to touch the surface of the workpiece.

Because of these problems I began to think of a hook-tool where the cutting part could be set to different positions in relation to the tool shank.

I started my experimenting by making small hooks, 40mm (1⅝in) long out of 4mm (⁵⁄₃₂in) round steel rods and attached them to a 12mm (½in) diameter shank. The tool worked, but making those small hooks was rather difficult, so I returned to the ring-tool and found that with a little adjustment I got the tool I was looking for.

The cutter or ring is fairly easy to make, even in HSS, and can be set to a lot of different positions (Photo 6). This enables the tool to cut in any direction – forwards, backwards and sideways.

As mentioned before, the ring is a bit limited as shavings sometimes get stuck in the ring. This is why I have persuaded C.I. Fall to make a very strong hook in HSS for the ring-tool grip (Photo 7).

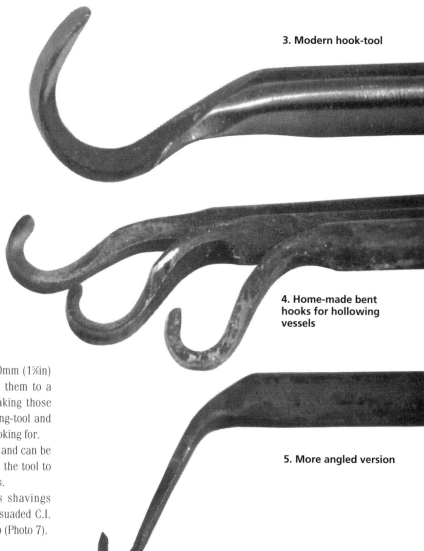

3. Modern hook-tool

4. Home-made bent hooks for hollowing vessels

5. More angled version

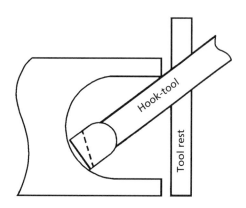

Fig 1 Hook-tool with internal bevel tends to dig in when hollowing small vessels

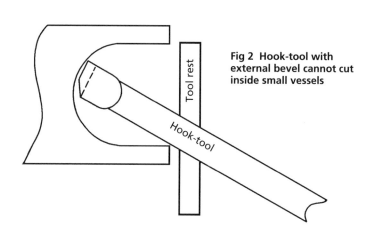

Fig 2 Hook-tool with external bevel cannot cut inside small vessels

As a result we now have a tool with three different cutters, 16mm (⅝in) and 25mm (1in) diameter rings and a very strong hook.

New tool

Another new tool that does not look like a hook-tool but works like a hook, is the tool shown in Photo 8. This tool with its exchangeable 18mm (²³⁄₃₂in) diameter HSS cutter, is much stronger than a straight hook and much easier to make. It is the perfect tool for egg-cups and goblets.

Photo 9 shows the original ring-tool at work on a piece of pearwood. As you can see, the tool is too short and therefore hard to use, but it cuts all right.

Photo 10 shows a bent hook at work on the same piece of pearwood, the tool cutting fast and efficiently.

Photo 11 shows the same tool as in Photo 5. Note that the tool is held so that the cutting takes part at the lowest section of the workpiece. A dig in at this point just lifts the tool off the workpiece with no harm done.

Photo 12 shows the ring-tool and how it is held when turning. It is easy for shavings to get stuck in the ring.

Photo 13 shows the adjustable hook-tool in use, the shavings just flying away from the tool and also away from the turner.

Photo 14 shows the same tool with the hook down under which makes the tool even more efficient.

Photo 15 shows the tool from Photo 8 at work. The tool can be used as a drill to open up the centre of the workpiece. Subsequently the tool can be pushed or pulled (Photo 16).

When turning a shallow bowl or hollow the tool is pushed and when turning a deeper and narrow object like a goblet the tool is pulled from the centre of the workpiece and up to the rim.

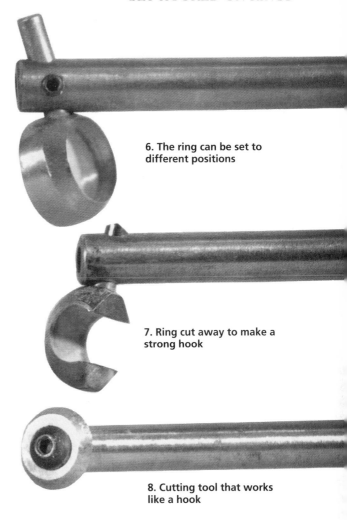

6. The ring can be set to different positions

7. Ring cut away to make a strong hook

8. Cutting tool that works like a hook

9. Original ring-tool cutting

10. Bent hook cuts better

11. The angled version from Photo 5 cutting

12. How the ring-tool is held

13. Adjustable hook-tool cutting well

14. Same tool with the hook held down cuts even better

15. The tool from Photo 8 at work

16. The tool being pulled

17. Hollowing with the original ring-tool

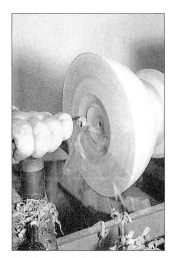

18. Standard straight hook at work

19. Ring-tool clogged with shavings

20. Adjustable hook-tool at work

The surface after turning is perfectly smooth and no sanding is needed. Normally I just polish the turned surface using some shavings.

Hollowing in cross-grain is first demonstrated with the original ring-tool from Photo 1. As mentioned before, the tool is too short and difficult to use (Photo 17).

Photo 18 shows a standard straight hook at work. The hook works quite well but it is a bit awkward to use as the turner has to lean away over the lathe in order to use the tool in a proper way.

On a pole lathe the hook-tool is used pointing downwards taking a slicing cut. The stance can be seen in *Drechsein in Holtz* by Steinert.

Photo 19 shows the 25mm (1in) at work, with shavings stuck in the ring, and Photo 20 shows the adjustable hook-tool at work. The shavings come off the workpiece very nicely – note the width of the cut and the size of the shavings.

Photos 21–23 show some of my turnings produced using the adjustable hook and ring-tool.

Photo 21 shows a jar in *Pinus contorta* hollowed out in end grain, height 340mm (13½in).

Photo 22 shows a jar 360mm (14¼in) high hollowed out in spalted alder, and Photo 23 shows a jar 160mm (6¼in) high turned in pine (*Pinus sylvestris*) turned and hollowed out in cross grain. Undercutting the rim was no problem using the adjustable ring-tool.

This article originally appeared in *Woodturning* issue 14, May/June 1993.

21. *Pinus contorta* jar 340mm (13.5in) high

22. Spalted alder jar 360mm (14.25in) high

23. Pine jar 160mm (6.25in) high

Get an edge

Sharp tools are essential to good woodturning. Here Dave explains how to get good edges on straight-ended tools, curved gouges, skews and cranked tools.

Dave Regester

Learning to turn is easy when you have at hand a good teacher who tells you not only how, but also why the tools can be manipulated to produce the shapes you have in your head. Unfortunately it gets harder when you get back to your own workshop and you do not have the reassuring hand of an expert to subtly alter the angles the tools are presented to the work.

You can deal with this problem if you have been taught why the tools cut and how to work it out for yourself, as all my pupils are. But what do you do if, however hard you try, you cannot produce the long curly shavings you managed on your course, and things are getting progressively worse. As a last resort you sharpen the tools!

Tool sharpening is as difficult to master as turning the wood, and the problem is that as you practise sharpening your tools they lose the shape that worked so well when you were being taught. Then, when things go wrong, you do not know whether it is because of the tools or what.

That is why in my book *Woodturning: Step by Step* I describe in some detail the way tools are sharpened, and illustrate in line drawings and photographs the shapes of tools I use.

There are those who indulge in discussions about the best way of sharpening tools – whether to use this or that arcane and time-consuming method.

You can safely ignore all this, take my word for it, and go for a nice cheap bog standard bench grinder with two wheels as wide as you can afford. Fit it with one soft, white aluminium oxide stone 60 to 80 grit, medium to soft grade K for high-speed steel tools, and one coarse grey stone for drastic work on carbon steel tools.

Most work can be done with your tools straight from the grinder.

Position the grinder as near the lathe as possible so there is no excuse for not using it, and put it on a shelf at about shoulder height if possible. Then you can use it without bending your back and can easily look at the side of the tool while sharpening to check the angle of the bevel.

Safety

During grinding small particles are produced which, if not contained, can penetrate into areas where they are not wanted – be careful not to get sparks in your eyes.

Only use a grinder that has a safety guard and always grind with it in place. The sort of transparent plastic shield you can see in the photographs stops most of the sparks from escaping, but some can be deflected into your eyes, so it is important to wear eye protection.

I always wear a Racal Airstream helmet while working and this affords excellent protection while grinding. If you do not use a helmet, safety goggles are vital.

As you can also see, my wheels are encased. This is because the wheel can disintegrate while rotating and bits of flying stone are best avoided.

Always use the rim of the wheel, not the side. If you use the side this can weaken the stone and cause it to disintegrate.

General tips

Do not press the tool onto the stone as this can cause it to overheat. If the tool changes colour you have altered the temper and this is not advisable.

If you need to do a lot of grinding because you want to alter the profile or get rid of chips on the edge, you do not do it any quicker by pressing harder.

1. Presenting a straight chisel flat on the rest at 90° to the wheel

2. Grinding the back bevel by presenting the chisel at an angle

3. First, a double bevel is produced.

visible on the bevel running at right angles to the edge. On a well-ground tool these striations will run from the edge to the shoulder, where the bevel meets the body of the tool, and there will be no facets visible on the bevel. That's something to aim for anyway.

When you grind a tool you should start at the shoulder and grind away until you get to the edge, when sparks will be seen going over the edge rather than underneath it.

You can tell when a tool is sharp by looking at the edge in bright light. If you can see light reflecting from the edge, it is not sharp. Always grind the whole of the edge of the tool, not just the bit that is blunt so that you preserve the profile.

How you stand at the grinder is as important as how you stand at the lathe. You need to be balanced so you do not have to shuffle around while you are moving the tool about.

If, before you turn on the grinder, you practise what you need to do so that every part of the edge passes over the rim of the stone (so the striations are produced at right angles to the edge) you can

4. Finally, the bevels combine to produce just one.

Heat can still build up during a long slow grind, so dipping it in water will prevent a loss of temper.

In the process of using the wheel, the rim will inevitably lose its flatness and become impregnated with steel and other rubbish. It will then need dressing, either with a star-wheel stone dresser or a dressing stone.

You might as well buy one of these when you buy the grinder because it is essential to keep the rim of the stone in good condition so it works efficiently.

Most turning tools need concave bevels so the bevel can rub the work to support the edge. This is naturally produced by the rim of the wheel if you present the tool to it so that the edge of the tool is more or less at right angles to the edge of the wheel (Photo 1).

In other words, the striations produced by the stone will be

work out where you need to stand at the beginning and end of each pass of the tool. Position yourself so that at the start of each pass your weight is on one foot and at the end it is on the other. If you can do the whole of an edge in one smooth swing you stand a good chance of getting a smooth bevel.

You can practise tool techniques on pieces of wood for as long as you like, but the problem with practising tool sharpening is that if you get it wrong you can lose the bevel angle and edge profile and you have got nothing left to copy.

It is some help if you have pictures of the tool shape, but it is a good idea to practise the basics of tool sharpening on an old chisel before you tackle the more complex shape of a turning tool.

Most of us have an old chisel around that we have regretfully abused and could well be converted into a square-ended scraper, perhaps for cutting the recess in the base of a bowl to accept an expanding chuck.

Basic skills

If you follow my instructions for converting this you will gain the basic skills of grinder use and be more qualified to tackle a more complex turning tool.

Square-ended chisels are the easiest tools to sharpen because there are no curves to mess up, but the lessons you learn are relevant to more complex shapes.

For a start, you will probably find the chisel is wider than the rim of the wheel. This means you will need to move the chisel across the rim in a steady side-to-side movement that covers the whole of the edge of the tool equally.

If the chisel is badly chipped you will need to grind the chips away, and it does not really matter at what angle you do this because all you need to establish at this stage is an edge without chips.

This allows you to concentrate on not pressing the tool too hard against the stone and regularly dipping the end in water to keep it cool. As already mentioned, it is best to use the coarse grey wheel for this, but in the photos I have used the white stone because it was easier to photograph.

When you have established a clean edge you can think about making a usable scraper by grinding the bevel to the appropriate angle.

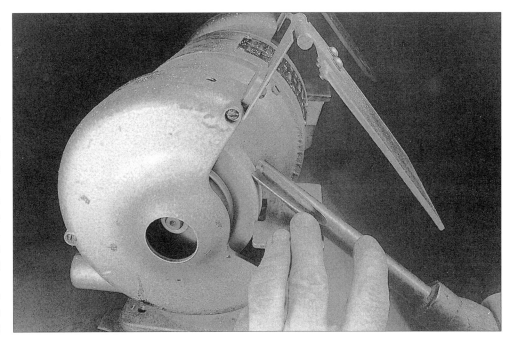

5. Sharpening the deep-fluted bowl gouge

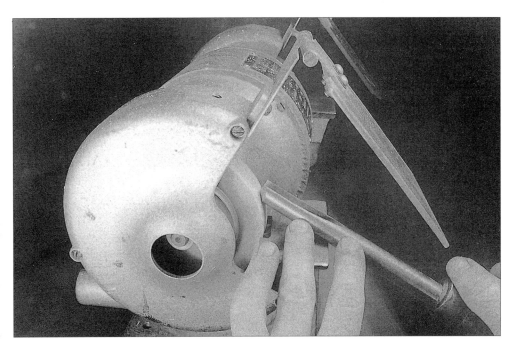

6. Edge ground straight across

I do not have any faith in the theory that scrapers rely for their ability to cut on the burr produced by the grinding process. I prefer to grind a bevel on my scrapers of about 60° and use the edge to cut because I do not think the burr lasts for any appreciable length of time when pushed against a rotating piece of wood.

To achieve this degree of bevel the tool needs to be presented to the wheel at an angle similar to that in Photo 2. The bevel should be started at the shoulder end with the tool passing to and fro across the wheel rim until you achieve a double bevel as in Photo 3.

This process is continued until sparks come over the edge of the tool and the bevels combine until you have only one, as in Photo 4.

Technique

Once you have mastered this technique you can progress with little trouble to sharpening other chisels such as the beading and parting tool and the traditional straight-edged skew.

The only additional problem that occurs with sharpening these is that bevels on both sides should be at the same angle and the edge should be at the correct angle to the tool. This just requires a little patience and a readiness to stop and examine what you have done at every step of the way.

Sharpening gouges and skews

Sharpening gouges and skews with a curved edge requires additional techniques. Once you have practised on a square-ended chisel and have mastered the smooth side-to-side movement necessary to get a consistent bevel of the angle desired (I

The roughing gouge is usually ground straight across but you must be sure that in the course of a succession of sharpenings you do not grind more from the centre of the edge than the corners. This can result in the corners of the tool projecting beyond the middle and thereby being in danger of catching in the work.

The rolling movement necessary to sharpen this tool is also used when turning, and it involves the tool being held on the rest of the lathe or the grinder with one hand in such a way that it is free to rotate between the fingers.

The rotating motion is imparted by the other hand in such a way that the grip does not have to be changed halfway through the movement. In other words at the start of the rotation the tool is held with the wrist rotated as far as possible in one direction so

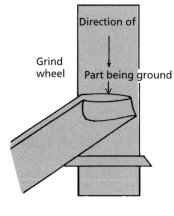

Fig 1 Moving the tool tip on the stone to grind the bevel

Grind wheel

Direction of

Part being ground

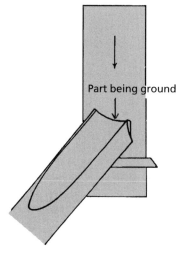

Fig 2 The tip is rolled round...

Part being ground

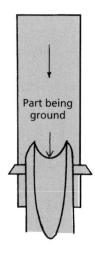

Fig 3 ...until the centre is reached.

Part being ground

recommend 60°) you can progress to sharpening a beading and parting tool and a traditional straight-edged skew.

The angle of bevel is largely a matter of personal preference and relates to factors such as your height and whether you have to manoeuvre your tools over the lathe bed. If the angle is too steep the edge will be too thick to cut cleanly, but if it is too shallow the edge will be so thin it will quickly overheat and become blunt.

Every so often I realise my bevels have become too short, usually as a result of the wheel on the grinder having worn down to too small a diameter. So I lengthen the bevel and suddenly it feels as if I have a new tool.

Roughing gouge

Sharpening a roughing gouge is not much more difficult than sharpening chisels. Instead of moving the tool smoothly from side-to-side you need to roll the tool so the whole of the edge passes across the rim of the wheel with the edge at right angles to the side of the wheel.

This has the effect of making sure the striations produced by the wheel run from the edge to the shoulder in a regular way and that the bevel is concave with the same curve as the outside of the wheel.

that when the tool is rotated it is the wrist that does the work, not the fingers.

In the photographs you will notice only the tips of the fingers of my left hand are in contact with the tool. This is because most of the work of directing the tool is carried out by my right hand – my left-hand fingers are merely acting as stops.

You may also notice the third finger of my left hand is very close to the stone. I did not notice I did this until after I had taken the photos. It is not necessary for it to be this close – indeed, it could be dangerous if you are not very careful and do not want your finger sharpened.

I have been using this grinder for 17 years and know it so well that I know by sheer familiarity how close my fingers can get without damage.

Deep-fluted bowl gouge

These tools are supplied with an edge ground more or less straight across and are sharpened in much the same way as the roughing gouge if this edge is to be preserved (Photos 5 and 6).

As you may notice, however, the angle of the bevel is not exactly the same along the whole of the edge. It is steeper at the bottom of

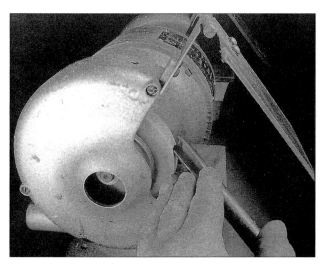

7. Grinding the sides first

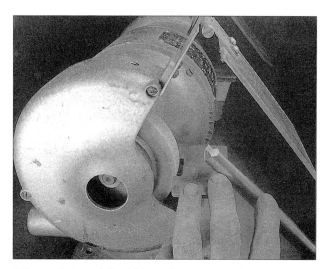

8. Two points are left which have to be ground away.

the flute than at the ends of the edge, which means as you approach the centre of the edge the handle end must be raised so the tool tip is lowered.

This is a typically gradual movement because the change in bevel angle is also gradual and it is in the mastery of such gradual movements that you can measure your progress.

If you wish to convert your straight-across gouge to the ground back type which gives you so many extra options in bowl turning both on the outside and inside of bowls, then you will need to grind back the wings.

Do both sides with the edge parallel to the rim of the stone and 45° to the vertical (Photo 7). When you have ground back both sides, with the edge of the tool parallel to the rest, and so the bevel on the sides is the same angle as the original bevel, you will have two points on each side which need to be ground away (Photo 8).

You are merging the side bevels into the old bevel, the last vestiges of which remain at the bottom of the flute, so this requires

Fig 4 Skew with curved edge

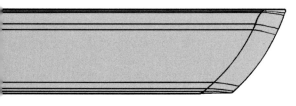

some delicacy and frequent stops to inspect what you have achieved.

Start by grinding at the point and then swinging the tool in an ever-greater arc either side of this point. Photo 9 shows the bevels partly merged, and Photo 10 shows the bevels on one side completely merged with the centre bevel. Now the other side needs to be done.

When you come to sharpen this tool subsequently you will have to swing it right from one side of the grinder to the other because you have to sharpen the entire edge, even though it may be blunt at only one point. You do not want to lose the profile.

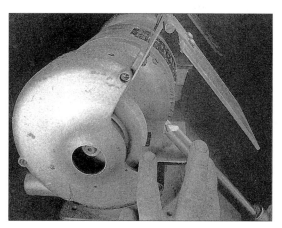

9. Bevels partly merged

10. Bevels on one side completely merged

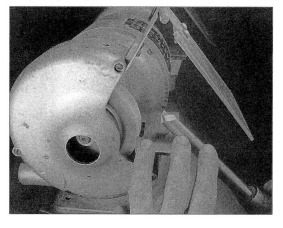

If you do as I recommended earlier and try the movements necessary to achieve this before switching on the grinder, you will see it is necessary to pass the tool between the grinder and your body.

11. Curving the skew.
Grinding the heel bevel

12. Grinding away
the point between
bevels

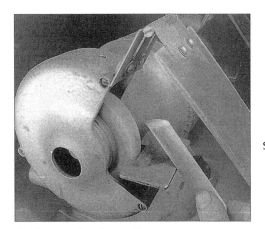

13. The completed smooth
curve

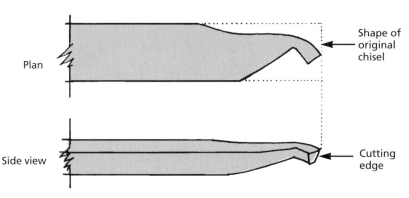

Plan

Side view

Shape of
original
chisel

Cutting
edge

Fig 5 Grinding a cranked tool
from a straight chisel

The secret of this smooth motion is the same as when sharpening the roughing gouge, that is gripping the bottom of the tool handle at the start of the movement with the wrist fully cocked and rotating the wrist as you go so that there is no need to change the grip halfway along.

In Figs 1, 2 and 3 I show how this complex movement makes the tool tip move at the stone for the left side and the centre of the bevel.

Curving the skew

I favour a skew chisel with a curved edge as in Fig 4 because it is easier to use and more versatile than the common straight-edged tool as supplied by the manufacturers.

The conversion job is not difficult and is shown in the sequence of Photos 11, 12 and 13. You start by grinding the bevel back on both sides and at the heel of the tool, so you end up with an edge that comes to a point half way along (Photo 11).

When you have four straight bevels of more or less the same width you then get rid of the point in the middle to make the edge into a curve (Photo 12) by moving the skew over the rim of the stone in a smooth arc. Photo 13 shows what you are aiming for.

Cranked tools

There is no great secret to making cranked tools; indeed, my ignorance about metalworking is so profound that they have to be simple to do or they are beyond me.

The way to make them without wasting tool steel would be to bend them, which would involve heating them to a great temperature and then tempering them when they have cooled down. The easy way is to convert a straight chisel by grinding the right angle out using the right angled edge of the stone as your guide (Fig 5).

Once you have learnt by practice to sharpen the normal tools consistently you can think of the tools as supplied merely as the starting point for you to make into the tools that work best for you.

Your tool sharpening will progress hand in hand with your turning skills, and the only limit to what you can achieve is your own imagination.

The Racal Airstream helmet is available from Isaac Lord, High Wycombe.

This article originally appeared in two parts, in *Woodturning* issues 14 and 15, May/June 1993 and July/August 1993.

Copy turning

Duplication, or copy turning, is a basic skill
which all woodturners should have, says Ernie,
as he outlines some tricks to help you along.

Ernie Conover

Duplication, or copy turning, seems to be a formidable problem to most turners. In fact, one of the most frequent questions I am asked is, 'What is the best duplicator to buy for my lathe?'

In case you do not know, a duplicator, or copying attachment, is an auxiliary carriage bolted onto a lathe bed. A knife connected to a pantograph travels freely on the carriage. A master part is placed between centres in the duplicator. This is usually at the front of the lathe. A billet of the appropriate diameter is placed between the actual centres of the lathe. The pantograph then traces the master and moves the knife proportionally.

Obviously this only works for spindle turning. While industrial quality duplicators have sophisticated knives that cut tangentially, the type we mere mortals can afford makes a simple scrape cut which leaves a finish that is nothing to brag about.

Duplicators are great for medium production runs, but short production runs are handled fine and dandy with just plain hand turning. Good hand turning with good basic techniques, that is.

Therefore, my answer to the above question is always, 'You are the best duplicator for your lathe.' While most folk take this for my usual wisecracking, it is one of the few times I am not being the least bit facetious.

On the assumption I am joking, the turner enumerates a plethora of excuses why he finds a duplicator absolutely necessary. Over the years I have distilled all this down to a basic truth – duplicator dependence boils down to lack of confidence and a

These turned columns on my house are not the same, but no one has ever mentioned it.

twentieth century space-age bent that 'alike' means plus or minus one micron.

Turning 100 things alike is a basic skill. If you have the skill to turn in the first place, you have the skill to duplicate. Like any other skill there are some tricks that can help tremendously. So here we will look closely at duplication. Not too closely, however, for no two hand-turned items will be exactly alike, just nearly alike.

Go into any antique store, callipers in hand, and take a close look at some pre-machine-age furniture. Chances are you will be hard put to find any two turned parts exactly alike. Some further study will even turn up some obvious discrepancies you didn't notice at first.

Symmetry

The human eye has such a passion for symmetry that it will make things uniform even if they are not. This phenomenon is the stock in trade of the magician. Not magic at all, illusion capitalises on your mind's mania to complete a task. Remove from your mind the impediment that any two pieces have to be *exactly* alike, for they just have to be nearly alike.

Philosophy aside, however, nothing replaces good workmanship. Hand turning, when executed with first-class workmanship, yields turning detail that no machine can duplicate. Good hand turning exhibits such things as undercuts and grooves at each edge of a bead which give a special crisp look to each piece. I elaborated on these details in my article on design in *Woodturning*, Issue 8, 'The Yin and Yang of Woodturning'.

Any woodturner worth his salt should be able to execute a production run of up to about 50 pieces with little trouble, even beating a duplicating lathe when setup is taken into account.

Nothing promotes precise duplication more than good basic techniques. Sheer cutting techniques that leave surfaces that require a minimum of sanding. Excessive sanding, the mark of a scraped turning, removes all the crispness you have worked so hard for. But aside from actual turning techniques, there are a gaggle of ideas that will help to duplicate parts.

Any turning will tend to have a maximum diameter at one, or more often several, points along its length. Since most turnings start from a square billet, this is a diameter that just brings it round. For example, with decent centring on 50mm (2in) stock, you will just turn round at about 48mm (1⅞in) give or take a millimetre. You do not need callipers to measure this: your roughing-out gouge (and your hands occasionally touching the revolving work) will tell you when things just come round.

I generally turn the entire length of the piece to this major diameter. Once I have established the major diameter I use callipers to find other diameters.

Using callipers

Callipers are a basic turning aid and when duplicating parts you can never have enough of them. I comb flea markets for callipers and regularly find top-quality ones made by Starrett, Greenlee and Stanley for $2.50 per pair. I probably have 25 pairs.

1. Using callipers with a cutoff tool

2. Using an open-ended wrench or spanner to size a tenon

3. Set of Buck Brothers gouges

For a production run I turn a master part and place it behind my lathe so it is available for visual reference. I then set a pair of callipers for each critical dimension. For small turnings I just set them out in order. For long turnings I hang them by the turning at the place they measure. I know turners who even colour code their callipers by placing coloured tape on the master piece and the callipers.

If the design will allow it I use callipers in combination with a cutoff tool. While slicing into the work with the cutoff tool held in my right hand I constantly monitor the progress with the callipers held in my left hand (Photo 1). When the calliper just drops over the work I know I am at the correct diameter.

Some care should be exercised here, for it is possible for the callipers to bind up in the slot you are chiselling in the work. If this happens they can go flying, with dire results. Always use a cutoff tool that is substantially wider 1mm (½₂in) than the callipers. Hold the callipers with a firm grip and do not force them over the work; allow them to naturally drop over.

Finally, stand just to one side of the cut so if they do go flying they will fly by you. Where a cutoff tool cannot be used with the callipers, I just turn with the appropriate tool and use the callipers to constantly monitor progress.

I also keep a set of inexpensive open-end wrenches or spanners hanging at the lathe. I use them as callipers for sizing tenons to specific drill sizes (Photo 2). Since an open-end wrench is slightly larger than an equivalent drill, I end up with a tenon that is a press fit.

This trick is a big time-saver because the wrenches are always set and ready to go. My friend Leo Doyle taught it to me. He even advocates forcing the wrench a bit at the last moment so as to compress the wood fibres of the tenon a bit. When water-based glue is applied the tenon swells, ensuring a 'get the hammer to take it apart' fit.

I have found most turnings have the above-mentioned major diameter and a readily apparent minor diameter. If you establish the major diameter by turning round and the minor diameter with callipers, everything else can be done by eye.

The trick here is to play the same theme from piece to piece. If you use the same gouge to make the cove or bead, the diameters will naturally come out close. The viewer's eye will pick up great discrepancies in the major and minor diameters, but not much else. What the eye does pick up is discrepancies in the height of various elements on each turning. This problem can be overcome through the use of masking tape, dividers and story sticks.

For short spindles (ones that do not require the tool rest to be moved) a piece of masking tape across the tool rest is a direct technique that works well. Pencil lines are drawn at the critical points so that elements may be placed quickly.

Tape works grand with one-time production runs of up to about 15 pieces. Above this the tape wears out before the job – not a good situation. If it is a routine job you do regularly, the tape leaves no record for the next time the job will be done.

Likewise, dividers (also found at bargain basement prices at flea markets) are handy for stepping off critical lengths along a spindle. By using several sets each element may be stepped off from the last. An additional advantage is that dividers both step off the distance and mark the work.

As with callipers, some care should be exercised when using dividers. Always rest both ends of the divider on the tool rest and do not overhang the tool rest too far (no more than 6mm (¼in)).

Never contact to anything but round work and only with a light touch. Contacting square work can make two sharp divider points go flying. As with tape, the drawback is that there is no stored record.

For longer work and repetitive jobs the best method of placing elements is with a story stick. A story stick is made by cutting notches in a thin strip of wood (1.5mm x 25mm (¹⁄₁₆in x 1in)) which match the critical points in the turning (Fig 1). This can be done with a tenon saw, a band or scroll saw or even a jack knife at a pinch.

Once the work is turned round the story stick is balanced on the tool rest. By placing a pencil or a scriber in each of the notches in turn the information is transferred. Story sticks are most noteworthy for jobs that are run repeatedly. The stick and a sample part may be filed away. When the time comes to run the job again they provide a splendid pattern.

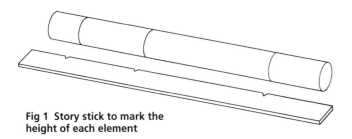

Fig 1 Story stick to mark the height of each element

Some turners put headless pins filed to a point in the story stick instead of cutting notches. Marking the wood like this saves having to use a pencil.

Tools for duplication

Tools are a great help in duplication – especially gouges. Each gouge will optimally cut a particular sweep of cove or bead. I treasure an old set of Buck Brothers gouges made around 1915. Three of the four were new when I found them – only the largest one had ever been handled. Unfortunately this one has seen quite a bit of wear, but the other three are beauties (Photo 3).

By employing the appropriate size gouge, depending on the sweep of the cove or bead I am turning, it is easy to achieve the same theme. The moral: match the tool to the job.

There are quite a few gimmicks sold, all promising easy duplication. These range from special shaped scrapers to semaphores. Semaphores are no more than a series of adjustable toggles mounted on a beam behind the work. They rest on the work and drop over centre when the critical diameter is reached. In my experience they would be useful only on a long-running job. They usually take more time to set and adjust than it takes to do the turning.

Special ground scrapers are another case. There are, of course, instances where only a scraper can get the job done. In this case we are talking real scraping where the tool is presented downhill and the cutting is done with a burr.

I have often ground a special tool to achieve a unique shape. I first read of the practice as a boy in a very old turning book. The project was to scrape a bracelet in the shape of the face of Queen Victoria.

I use special scrapers regularly to make captive rings. I will grind a matched pair of left and right from an old file. Such tools are now sold commercially for those who do not want to bother making them. Sorby sells captive ring scrapers in three sizes.

Finally, in this age of CD disc recordings, why do people still flock to live performances? They go because they enjoy the *reality* of a mistake or two. Take 1,000 people off the street and

Windsor chair made from green wood by master chairmaker Michael Dunbar. He takes about nine minutes to turn each leg.

examine their belongings. They possess mass-produced articles, and it is hard to find one with something truly unique.

I think the reason many of us are drawn to turning is the ability to make something that is both beautiful and unique. As a hand craftsperson go out of your way to impress upon whoever you give, sell or show your work to that it is truly hand-made. That they *will* find some variation. Point out to them that in this plastic age you are offering something truly unique. Make sure, however, that the turnings are only slightly different from one another, not a series of one-of-a-kind originals.

This article originally appeared in *Woodturning* issue 15, July/August 1993.

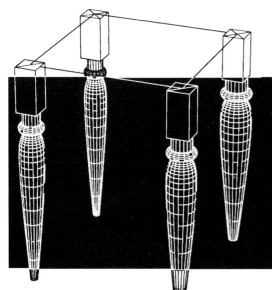

Fig 2 Nearly alike. A 3D computer-aided design drawing of four table legs set 355mm (14in) on square. After generating three copies of the first leg, I then scaled the turned portions up and down. The first I made 20% smaller, the second 10% smaller and the third 10% bigger. This is an overall difference of 30%. I then projected the drawing in perspective from a viewing point of 10 feet away and about head height. Can you see which are which? This is a much greater variation than you would normally have.

Seasoning secrets

Whether your wood is as dry as a bone or wringing wet when you work it, it has to dry sometime. Here are some basics to help you avoid disasters.

Bob and Ann Phillips

Wood is a marvellous medium in which to work. It offers warmth, tactile appeal, colour and strength. It also provides a high degree of frustration, as any woodworker who has experienced difficulties when seasoning timber can testify. The medium in which we work draws together a large family of craftsmen and artists, from cabinetmakers to carvers and turners. But the medium that links

our diverse talents also acts as a great leveller. If wood drying problems develop then even the best craftsmanship and artistic merit can be overturned.

We've all seen doors, drawers or lids which stick, gaps caused by shrinkage, or carvings marred by gigantic cracks. In short, those very attributes which attract us to work with wood can prove our undoing.

Whatever our field of woodworking, we share a common need for well-seasoned timber. Sometimes we can work unseasoned wood, but it still has to be dried for completion.

The advantages of using green, or wet, timber include lower costs, access to a greater diversity of timbers and sizes, and control of the seasoning process and hence of final quality.

When green (wet) wood dries out, the first moisture lost is the free water – water from the cell cavities not bound in any way. At this stage there is no shrinkage, even though large quantities of moisture are released from the wood.

1 and 2. This piece of resinous kaurl had a waxy coating applied to the figured area, which would have been likely to dry unevenly.

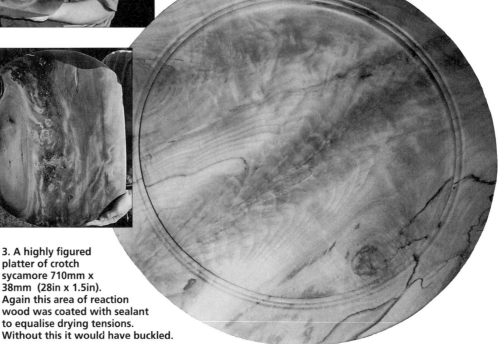

3. A highly figured platter of crotch sycamore 710mm x 38mm (28in x 1.5in). Again this area of reaction wood was coated with sealant to equalise drying tensions. Without this it would have buckled.

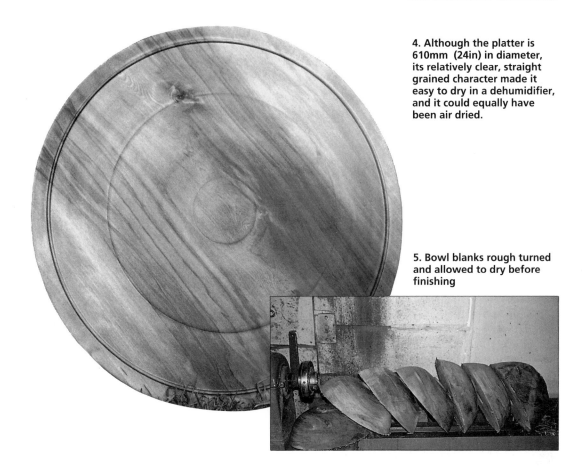

4. Although the platter is 610mm (24in) in diameter, its relatively clear, straight grained character made it easy to dry in a dehumidifier, and it could equally have been air dried.

5. Bowl blanks rough turned and allowed to dry before finishing

The next stage comes when all this free water has gone, and water starts to be lost from the wood cell walls, causing dimensional changes.

Seasoning defects

These changes don't occur equally in all directions, and because of this unequal shrinkage, tensions are set up. These cause the seasoning defects we'll now consider from the standpoint of keeping them to a realistically acceptable minimum.

Furniture makers have an easier, time since most work with stock widths of no more than 255mm (10in). The advantage is that tensions in wood are reduced in cutting from tree width down to plank width. Certainly cutting and jointing can be used to remove defects, but how much better to avoid the necessity of this extra work and waste.

Everything we will discuss for drying thick slabs (as might be required by carvers and turners) is made easier when considering plank form – particularly when thicknesses are not great, say 50mm (2in) or less.

Faults caused by poor drying technique are most often seen as slitting (or checking). Commonly end splits show at the board or block ends, and can prove to run a long way invisibly, causing cracking of a piece later on. The fault is brought about by the ends losing water at a faster rate than other parts of the wood.

In the old days exposed end grain was covered by battens of waste wood nailed on, and the modern equivalent is a moisture-retarding coating, directly applied. Our sealant of choice is a wax emulsion which we find effective and convenient, although paint and other sealants are commonly used.

Surface checking or splitting is another form of the problem and again is due to uneven water loss. As wood dries the water is lost first from the surface, then water gradually moves from the middle towards the outside.

Under good drying conditions this will have the effect of evening out the moisture content of the whole cross section of wood. If conditions are adverse, then drying stresses develop.

In air drying the solution is to cut down the airflow through your stack so that moisture loss is slowed. In a cabinet dryer, the humidity and temperature would be adjusted, possibly incorporating a high humidity treatment in the final stages of drying.

An allied problem which is common in kiln drying can also crop up in air drying if water is lost too rapidly. This could occur where you have sited a drying stack in a particularly sunny, windy spot, or you may simply be caught out by vagaries of climate.

The fault is called case-hardening, and indicates the outside (case) has dried out too rapidly to shrink normally and because of this some of the inside wood is stretched or under tension. All of this sets up some terrible stresses because the inside can't lose moisture evenly to shrink as it should.

This defect is in some ways the very worst. At least you can see defects like splitting, but with case hardening unless you had the foresight to try samples, the first indication of problems will be when you start to try to work the timber.

The compression/tension forces set up a kind of balance, and it is only when this 'controlled stress' is released by, say, planing or cutting to size that the balance is disturbed and warping results. Not too tragic perhaps for thin sections, but diabolical where you need thicker cross-sections.

Warping

Warping seen as a result of working case-hardened timber is a defect in its own right. There are various types of warping – bowing (resulting from warping along sides of planks or blocks), crooking and cupping (both resulting from warping along edges) and a variety of others. Our aim is to avoid these defects.

For these and allied defects the recipe for avoidance is much the same – well stacked timber on sound, even fillets (sticks to

6. Green turned bowls have their rims coated with sealant to prevent distortion when drying.

separate the slabs of timber). Air flow must be carefully considered when selecting a site for your drying stack, and protection given from overly rapid drying – use of shade, covers or sealants as appropriate.

In all cases use a moisture meter or take samples for weighing so you know the state of dryness of your wood.

A further feature, or defect (depending on your viewpoint) which you may come across when drying timber is the occurrence of localised distortion around knots, resin or pitch pockets and reaction timber (unusual grain patterns caused when trees have grown under stress).

Cabinet makers often select out clear boards of straight-grained timber. This makes life easier, since the clear timber has less tension and is more likely to season without difficulty. Where unusual features are acceptable, even sought after, we need to take particular care with drying methods to ensure a good result.

In the example of kauri timber (*Agathis australis*) in Photos 1 and 2 the area of high resin content which would have been likely to dry unevenly was coated with sealant before final seasoning and a stunningly unusual piece emerged. Kiln drying for such heterogeneous samples is often disastrous.

So far we have dealt with coping with problems which arise from drying wood too quickly. It is possible, however, to dry wood too slowly and encounter problems associated with moulds and fungi.

Fungal growth

One person's perceived defect is another's prized feature, and turners especially have been known to deliberately set up conditions suitable for fungal growth. In this way they encourage fungi to colour their wood for them by the discolouration of incipient decay.

If you find fungal growth becoming a problem on the surface of air-drying wood it is just a matter of increasing air movement through the stack to discourage the growth. Consider removing covers and increasing the air space between slabs.

In drying kilns operating at high temperatures, thermo-tolerant

7. Outdoor air drying of wood blocks. The end grain of each has been coated with sealant to slow water loss and the airflow reduced by a cover of horticultural cloth.

moulds can become a problem. But it is unlikely that small-scale dehumidifiers, which are in effect a variety of low-temperature kiln, would experience such infestation.

It is interesting that while many time-worn techniques can be handed down with advantage, there seem to be few useful guidelines for seasoning timber that translate usefully to modern requirements.

Historically, logs were placed in streams to wash out the sap, which is a great idea if you have a handy stream by you and have access to heavy lifting gear. But when do you pull it out? These wise saws are notoriously short on detail.

In a moment of madness we once bought a hefty hardwood log

which had been recovered from such a watery source. We really thought we were on to a gold mine.

It took weeks of frustrating labour to establish we'd bought, at best, a worked-out coal mine. The wood was irretrievably dulled and drastically weakened structurally. We still listen to colourful tales of yore but, like the timber, we're less green.

Moisture content

It follows from all this that when we select wood for our projects we need to give as much attention to moisture content as we do to more immediately apparent qualities such as colour and grain patterns.

We hope these guidelines will help you to reduce losses which you may have encountered when drying timber, and help you select the most appropriate conditions in which to dry different types.

A stack of basically clear slabs for example, especially if you've had the miller quarter-saw it for you, can generally be rapidly dried without problems where reasonable drying conditions are provided.

Highly figured slabs with a high content of reaction wood or other defects/features need special care taken to even out the drying process as we've discussed (sealing over areas most likely to distort and so on). This can enable you to season even the most awkward timbers.

8. Slabs of beech drying in our small dehumidifier / drying cabinet. Note the fillets to separate the slabs and permit airflow, also used when air drying.

In our own early days we probably wasted more timber due to poor drying practices than we dare think about. While woodworkers cannot hope to totally eliminate a degree of loss in the seasoning process, it is certainly possible to reduce these losses to the absolute minimum.

However we decide to dry our wet wood, the basic premise on which good seasoning procedure is based is that tension is created when water is lost from wood. By taking steps to minimise this tension we are able to dry timber in an economic and conservative way, even when the timber is highly figured.

A broad knowledge of the drying process enables us to provide suitable drying conditions so that drying defects are kept to a minimum. But we should state here that wood, like many living materials, has the ability to adapt to different surroundings. Even

well seasoned timber holds some moisture – the amount will depend not only on the timber and its characteristics but also on local conditions.

As stated above, wood loses free water at first. When the moisture content gets down to around 25–30% it reaches the shrinkage intersection point, which varies with different timbers. It is then that the bound water begins to be lost and dimensional changes such as shrinkage occur.

If wood is exposed long enough to constant temperature and humidity it will lose or gain moisture until a balance is achieved. When this happens the wood is said to have reached its equilibrium moisture content (EMC) for the conditions.

Each country has a standards authority which sets levels of acceptable wood moisture content for building regulations etc. These will differ with climate, but typically are set around 8–12% for interior work situations and 13–18% for exterior.

A wooden stool in your kitchen may have an EMC of 12%, but the same stool left for a year or so in an unheated shed or garage workshop could have a moisture content of 15%. So even 'dry' timber can take up moisture and lose it again to attain a balance with the humidity of its surroundings.

By now, the phrase 'dry as a bone' as used by retailers of wood should generate only scepticism and hollow laughter.

Methods

We can now take things a stage further by using this general information to help select the most appropriate of the specific drying methods we shall consider next.

First though, no matter whether you come down on the side of natural air drying or ultimately become converted to more rapid methods such as low-temperature kilns or even chemically assisted methods such as polyethylene glycol (PEG), you'll need to know how dry your timber is, if only to know when to stop!

There are two options here – measurement by weight or by electrical-resistance-type meters.

To determine moisture in wood by weighing you need only a set of scales and an oven. The drawbacks are that it takes a little effort, and you'll need to take test samples from your stock. However, if you don't object to spending a little time it is perfectly possible to make accurate determinations of wood moisture content.

Make sure your sample is truly representative of your timber stock. If you just lop off the ends for drying they're likely to be drier than the rest of the stock.

Weigh your sample promptly after cutting, ideally within a few minutes. You can seal samples in a plastic bag if it isn't possible to weigh them immediately.

With the wet weight recorded, dry the sample in an oven set at around 100° C and reweigh. When the successive weighings don't change you can record this dry weight and determine the weight of water lost from the sample.

The weight lost divided by the dried weight, all multiplied by 100 will provide the moisture content as a percentage figure – the conventional mode of expression.

Expressed as a formula, this is:

initial weight - ovendry weight   x 100 = % moisture content
          ovendry weight

As an example, taking a freshly cut piece of wood, if the sample initially weighed 100 gm and after drying weighed 52.5 gm, then using the above formula you calculate a moisture content of 90%. Or, in other words, the wet wood contained 47.5 gm as water.

Kitchen scales and ovens are not precision instruments so your measurements can't be as accurate as laboratory determinations, but they will be good enough for your purposes and will normally

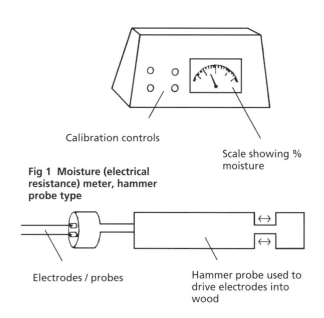

Calibration controls

Scale showing % moisture

Fig 1 Moisture (electrical resistance) meter, hammer probe type

Electrodes / probes

Hammer probe used to drive electrodes into wood

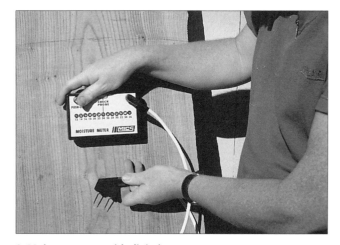

9. Moisture meter with digital type display, and probes

be as good or better than meter determinations.

One thing you should watch is that temperature isn't more than a few degrees over 100° C, otherwise more than water will be driven off.

The method is superior to meter readings in some ways. For example you can determine moisture contents outside the range measurable by meters. Most trees freshly felled have moisture levels around 100%, although a few, such as Western red cedar, can exceed 200%.

Moisture meters rely on wood being a better conductor, or less effective resistor, when it is wet. As wood dries the resistance rises until it can't be accurately measured further.

Meters are fine to measure moisture contents in the 5–35% range, but most are little use outside that range. The resistance offered by dry wood changes too little below this level to be measured.

There are meters available to measure over a wider range, but these are more expensive tools designed for research establishments, real state-of-the-art instruments with specially compensated and calibrated gadgetry.

We've had such specialised equipment on loan for specific tasks, but they would offer no real advantage to the average woodworker over the cheap, hand-held user-friendly meters with a nominal 1% accuracy.

As with the oven dryweight method you still need to take care to ensure good results.

Fig 1 and Photo 9 show the main parts of moisture meters. Smaller models have integral probes (electrodes). Often these are quite short, so that unlike the hammer-type probe, which is driven deep into the wood, the needle probes may only measure moisture content of the outermost layer of your wood.

A quick way around this is to hammer a couple of nails into the wood and connect the meter needles to these. Alternatively you could take a cut through the wood you wish to measure and test the moisture content of the core.

It is important you take the trouble to do this, as the moisture gradient effect means a thick slab of wood could register 10% near the surface yet still be at 20% at the centre.

Readings will be affected by species, by temperature and by coating (such as end sealants). In practical terms these aren't too troublesome. Some meters can be calibrated, others supply correction charts.

One last point – remember that electrical resistance is being measured, so avoid taking surface readings on misty mornings where surface moisture can affect the readings, unless your meter has insulated probes.

Either of these two methods provides you with the means to determine moisture content of wood. Even if you don't season your own stocks of timber you'll benefit from this ability.

Indeed, you may come to regard your moisture meter as one of the most useful tools you possess. Wood is not invariably as dry as it's claimed to be, and a moisture determination will reduce both uncertainty and price.

If you do season your own timber there is a range of choices as to how to go about it. We'll take the simplest first.

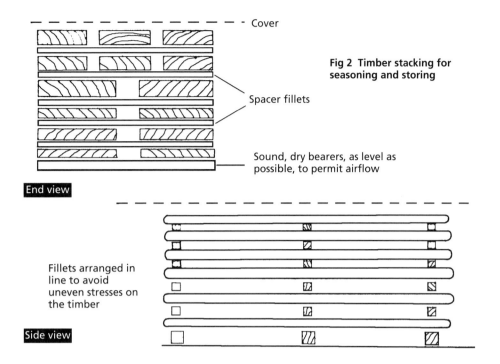

Cover

Fig 2 Timber stacking for seasoning and storing

Spacer fillets

Sound, dry bearers, as level as possible, to permit airflow

End view

Fillets arranged in line to avoid uneven stresses on the timber

Side view

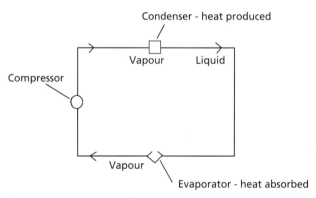

Condenser - heat produced

Vapour   Liquid

Compressor

Vapour

Evaporator - heat absorbed

Fig 3 Main components of a heat pump cycle

Air drying

Air drying is the method of choice of many woodworkers, and certainly the method we usually start with. Good stacking is basic to both air drying and kiln drying and we covered above the considerations to keep in mind to avoid drying defects or degrade.

The site for the timber stack should be level and stable, even if you have to lay a foundation of sorts to achieve this. Separate the timber slabs with dry fillets (sticks) placed in line above the stack bearers as shown in Fig 2. Ensure that end grain is sealed. There is endless scope for preferred size of fillets, type of cover for stacks and so on.

You'll know your own site best. Keep in mind the effect of drying on stresses that we've discussed and adapt your method to your situation.

Production timbers such as elm and straight-grained wood which dry readily can cope with 25mm (1in) fillets, spaced 900–1,000mm (36in–40in) apart, whereas a tricky customer, such as highly figured or resinous wood, may be safer stacked using thinner 12mm (½in) and close-spaced fillets, say 255–460mm (10in–18in) apart.

In a sheltered spot a few end slabs on top provide adequate cover, yet a stack in an open situation would need more effective cover. Exert as much control over conditions as you are able and air drying can be efficient as well as cheap.

Finally, and so easy to say, plan stack placement to avoid

moving the stack until you have to!

Fast-track seasoning

The most obvious drawback to air drying is time, but if you are well organised you will cope with this. Less readily resolved are problems that arise because of the lack of control over drying conditions. This can be very hard to cope with.

Probably the most economical way to season timber under controlled conditions is with a dehumidifier or heat pump drier.

Dehumidifiers and heat pump driers are attractive to small-scale woodworkers not least because of their low running costs when compared with conventional kiln driers. This economy is achieved by making use of the refrigeration cycle, providing an

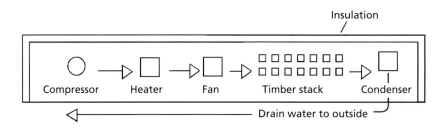

Fig 4 Main features of a dehumidifier

effective heat source for drying. (Conventional kilns vent heat outside the cabinet.)

Dehumidifiers and heat pump driers have many features in common, but dehumidifiers have the entire heat pump within the cabinet, and in order to remove the moisture which has come out of wood it must be condensed so it can be drained off as a liquid.

Both types of cycle are shown in Figs 3 and 4. There are variations on the theme, but in essence the warm air is recycled in a closed system so no extra energy (in the form of heat) is needed, provided the cabinet is well insulated.

On balance the dehumidifier unit can season timber rapidly (weeks rather than years as is the case with air drying) and being energy efficient in design, costs little to operate.

Depending on what is available locally, and your capabilities, you could either purchase a complete unit or have one tailor-made to your own design as we did (Photos 10 and 11). We don't have space to go into detail, but we had made up a dehumidifier-type unit to the outline system illustrated.

By monitoring airflow, humidity, temperature at all points within the drying cabinet during operation (using high-tech equipment lent by the Ministry of Forestry) we were able to identify any inefficiencies in the prototype and so design an efficient drying system that we now consider essential.

Our well insulated cabinet is self-contained. Warm air from the compressor is pushed through the stacked timber by the fan. In our case we haven't needed to use a heater, but an outside cabinet or one less well insulated may need such a booster.

Once the cycle is established it is self-sustaining – and we can use the leached water on our tomatoes.

With this dehumidifier we can dry a cubic metre of green wood in less than a month, and it costs only as much as a domestic fridge to run.

Since first playing with prototypes several years ago, we have made larger models from the same design which are now used by cabinetmakers for drying their own stock and drying timber to sell to others.

Dehumidifiers can be used with green bowl turning, but as there are so many variables (wall thickness, initial moisture content, temperature/humidity settings etc.), each user will need to experiment with their own equipment.

Using a drier of this sort enables you to control the factors which affect timber seasoning – airflow, temperature and relative humidity.

Air drying is cheap, but losses can sometimes be unacceptably high due to the uncontrolled nature of the seasoning. A sudden unexpected climatic change such as a hot, drying wind can prove devastating to quality timber stacked outdoors.

Air drying can also only bring wood to a moisture content in equilibrium with prevailing conditions.

The other drying methods we'll cover relate more to smaller-scale drying and are not applicable to all woodworkers.

Green bowl turning

Strictly speaking, this is a mixture of methods since the part-working of the wood is followed by air drying or a fast-track method.

Turners have their own pet methods which seem to work more or less well, so the technique described is suggested rather than dogmatically laid down. What's involved is removing wood you don't need before you start seasoning. The wet (green) blanks are turned to a thickness to allow for distortion, and the part-finished bowl is dried. The dried bowl-form is put back on the lathe for finishing and that's all!

There are many roads to the final goal, and, for what it's worth, we generally turn initially to a wall thickness of 25mm (1in) and seal the rim and highly figured parts. Huge bowls we encase in semipermeable bags and if we need them quickly they go into the dehumidifier!

PEG

Polyethylene glycols form a series of high molecular weight polymers which are astonishingly useful bulking agents in cosmetics, foodstuffs, coatings and other applications where their low toxicity and bulking properties are appropriate. They are available as solids, flakes or in solution.

The number usually shown with each indicates approximately the molecular weight and therefore size. PEG 1000 is useful for timber treatment and, indeed, has been useful for conditioning ancient wooden artifacts to changing conditions, e.g. when dredged up from historic sites.

The material is expensive and would be unlikely to be a method of choice for many woodworkers. The method we used was quite successful, although messy and inconvenient. Here's how.

Dissolve the PEG flakes in water at the rate of 1lb/425gm per litre of water. This gives a solution with a specific gravity 1.05. (Home brewers may find it simpler to adjust concentration using their hydrometer.)

The wood to be treated can now be immersed in the PEG solution. We have tried both solid timber and part-finished articles made of fruitwoods. Once used the solution can be brought back up to strength with added PEG and the procedure repeated.

A week-long soaking was effective for the small pieces we used, and certainly worked well for timbers known to be difficult to season otherwise.

American stores stock PEG 1400, which acts just as well as a bulking agent to treat wood but will take longer to diffuse into the wood. Some people leave wood in for ten days to ensure complete uptake.

One possible drawback is the waxy-impregnated end-product, but an oil/wax finish will give no problems.

Microwave drying

The amazing feature of this is the speed. The microwave energy is absorbed by the moisture in the wood. The individual water molecules vibrate millions of times per second and in so doing produce heat, giving water inside wood the energy to be driven out from the wood.

A suggested workable method for small turned objects is as follows: First, turn the form to near final size. For a small dish we aim for 6mm (¼in) wall and base thickness.

Microwave oven settings vary, so some experimentation will be needed to establish a routine for your own equipment. Start with a low power setting for several minutes. Ideally the heat will be enough to drive steam from the dish.

Dab excess moisture, cool, and repeat the treatment. You are aiming to drive out moisture quickly but not so severely as to distort the dish, which should never get too hot to handle. Next simply put back on the lathe for finishing.

More violent treatment can be applied deliberately to produce weird forms. It's all great fun.

Readers wishing to read further on the qualities and seasoning of wood should consult the books by Desch and Hoadley (see bibliography, p. 109).

This article originally appeared in two parts, in *Woodturning* issues 16 and 17, October 1993 and November 1993.

11. The dehumidifier stripped down

10. Our own dehumidifier unit ready for use in the drying cabinet. Controls and digital display unit are on the top.

German hoop turners' tools

How the traditional toymakers of Erzgebirge use specialist tools to cut hoops from wet end grain

Johannes Volmer

In the Erzgebirge – the 'ore mountains', Saxony border region of Germany – ancient woodturning techniques are still practised by toymakers and artisans. Among these methods, hoop turning requires the highest skill. This unique folk turning craft has been described in detail in German books by Hellmut Bilz.

In the process of hoop turning, the turner creates a ring that has the continuous profile of an object – for instance an animal – within it. The profile is mainly turned into the end grain of green wood with specific tools. These tools differ from usual tools (Photo 1). They facilitate the turning of smooth surfaces which need not be sanded,

A wooden hoop section for camels, with animals cut from other hoops

and besides, the surfaces of green wet wood cannot be cleaned well by sanding. That means that without exception the hoop turner's tools cut the wood fibres – there is no scraping at all.

Handling these tools requires a lot of training. For the observer and the beginner the tools seem extremely dangerous, but the skilled turner uses them very efficiently. He rapidly hollows the work by piercing the end grain and slicing the wood into thick, broad, endless shavings.

The origin of the tools

The tools are said to originate from mould turning in the ancient medieval Erzgebirge glassworks. The green wooden moulds were expected to be produced extraordinarily precisely and with glass-smooth surfaces. The expertise was handed down through the generations to the hoop turning toymakers of the last century. Their tools and lathes are exhibited in the Erzgebirge Toy Museum in Seiffen, a toy making centre to this day.

Numerous modifications of the tools are to be seen, since every turner had specially shaped and ground tools according to the range of objects he produced.

Although today's hoop turning artisans use tools forged from better steel, the geometry of their tools is just the same.

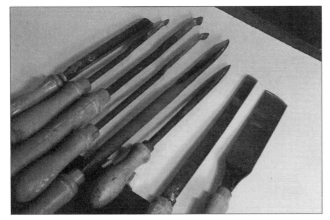

1. Range of tools used for hoop turning

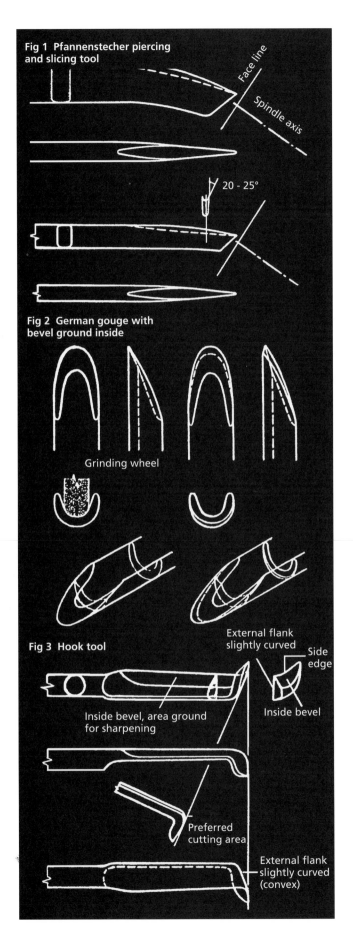

Fig 1 Pfannenstecher piercing and slicing tool

Face line

Spindle axis

20 - 25°

Fig 2 German gouge with bevel ground inside

Grinding wheel

Fig 3 Hook tool

External flank slightly curved

Side edge

Inside bevel

Inside bevel, area ground for sharpening

Preferred cutting area

External flank slightly curved (convex)

End grain tools

There are principally three kinds of end grain tools:

1 The Pfannenstecher, a piercing and slicing (peeling) tool (Fig 1).
2 The German gouge (Deutsche Rohre), a fluted gouge with the bevel ground inside (Fig 2).
3 The hook (Fig 3).

Each of these tools is available in a variety of shapes and sizes, and the usual gouges, skews, parting tools as well as spoon bits are also applied.

I will explain the application of these tools when turning a profile of a ring into end grain. A length of freshly cut spruce log or one which has been stored underwater is hammered onto the ring chuck and roughed out with a normal broad gouge. Then the work has to be faced off square with a strong skew curved chisel (Photo 2). Its bevels must be ground straight or convex but not at all concave (hollow) as this could easily cause heavy catches and tearing of the work.

The gouge and the chisel are supported by a standard tool rest that stands parallel to the spindle. The hoop turner also uses both these tools for shaping profiles on the perimeter of the work as with all centrework. The tools' edges have small sharpness (wedge) angles and must be controlled for best cutting (not scraping) conditions to obtain clean surfaces on the wet wood.

The Pfannenstecher

The initial cut into the end grain is done with the Pfannenstecher (Photo 3). Moving forward the tool's small circular edge, the spear point cuts the fibres at right angles. Going radially toward or away from the rotational axis, the lateral edges slice (peel) the wood into long shavings (Photos 4 and 5). This process is something like roughing down a work, and the surfaces obtained by the spear point are not evenly smooth.

The details of the hoop's profile must be shaped by cutting cleanly with the

2. A strong skew is used to square the end of the log.

German gouges and hooks. Both tools are moved through certain positions and, like the Pfannenstecher, may be safely pressed against the transversal tool rest (Photo 6).

The tool rest

This rest is made from a simple board with a cross-section of about 75mm x 25mm (3in x 1in) and chamfered and rounded on one side. It lies on the parallel tool rest mentioned above and stands with its

3. Pfannenstecher cuts into end grain.

6. The tool rest is placed across the surface of the workpiece for close cutting.

4 and 5. Long shavings are produced.

Wooden hoop section for giraffes

end on the base board of the lathe bed without being fixed.

The turner places the rest angled across the face of the work depending upon the tool he uses and its necessary cutting position. The rest remains standing upright since the contact force of the tool presses it against the work face. Too much pressure causes burning to the rest and to the work.

The elasticity of the wooden rest and its soft natural surface and chamfer have the tools easily controlled by the feel of the hands. However, the rest is quickly worn out and often has to be replaced.

The German gouge

The German gouge is a more or less deep fluted gouge with the bevel ground on the inside. In the Erzgebirge area it is used mainly for hollowing centrework, for roughing out and for finishing as well.

For turning narrow deep holes the gouge is also provided with an external bevel. This bevel yields – as with common gouges – better riding with the work's surface. A skilled turner completely hollows and finishes an egg cup, for example, with the German gouge by only four or five cuts.

When cutting profiled shapes into wet end grain the German gouge has to be controlled so that the wood fibres run at a slight angle against the edges, i.e. its round middle part or the less curved lateral parts.

Thus, obtaining clean surfaces by shearing cuts only is the essential aim in the art of operating the German gouge (Photos 7 and 8 and Figs 4 and 5).

'Without exception the hoop turner's tools cut the wood fibres – there is no scraping at all'

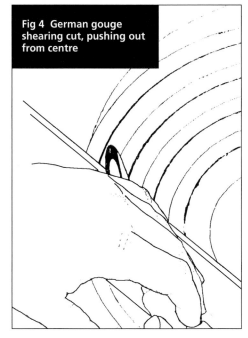

Fig 4 German gouge shearing cut, pushing out from centre

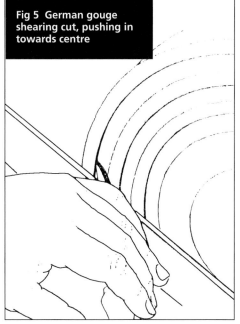

Fig 5 German gouge shearing cut, pushing in towards centre

7 and 8. Cutting with the German gouge

The hook

This substantial cutting condition must also be fulfilled when cutting with the hooks. They cut the fibres like a very small German gouge with the handle perpendicular to the usual handle position. That disposition of edge and handle allows you to get shearing cuts with the grain on places of the profile where the gouge would otherwise have to be inside the work (Photos 9–13).

The angle between the straight main edge of the hook and the side edge is nearly 90°. The radius of the round part of the edge, the nose, must be small for hollow (concave) profiles, with greater curvature or internal corners.

Fig 3 shows views of the typical end grain hook. The hooks differ from the angle between flanks of the main and the side edge, and they are differently strong. The nose is the mainly used cutting area.

In general the sharpness (wedge) angle of tools for roughing is greater than for finishing tools. The hoop turners mainly use spruce and for small objects lime, elder and birch. These softwoods require sharpness angles between 20° and 40°.

Roughing tools are longer and stronger and have longer handles. The German gouges and hooks for profiling the hoop and clean cutting are shorter due to the required manoeuvrability. But they must also be long for deeply profiled hoops, e.g. for a long-tailed bird or a giraffe.

Grinding and sharpening

Grinding and sharpening the gouges and hooks seems to be an art in itself. The turners use normal grinding wheels for the external areas of the tools, and they have small rounded and chamfered wheels for the internal concave parts of the tools (Fig 2). Among them are wheels with smaller diameters for grinding the spoonlike internal hollow sphere of the German gouges.

In order for wheels to be in action simultaneously there are up to six of them mounted and centred on one shaft in bearings on each end, easy to disassemble and belt-driven by a motor. In general the turners need no rest for grinding the tools.

Tourists can observe all processes of hoop turning with these uncommon tools in workshops open to the public. The Erzgebirge Toy Museum in Seiffen has restored for demonstration a water-wheel-powered mill erected in 1760.

Here visitors can get acquainted with the ancient craft in genuine surroundings. They enjoy the smells of resinous spruce, and admire the skilful handling of the hooks and the Pfannenstecher causing flying shavings several metres long.

This article originally appeared in *Woodturning* issue 16, October 1993.

Models made from hoops

9–13. Cutting with the hook tool

Cooked to a turn

The high cost of seasoned wood caused Helen Sanderson to turn to green wood and microwave seasoning. Here she pin-points the pleasures and pitfalls of 'cooking' wood in a standard microwave.

Helen Sanderson

For people working in wood the cost of raw materials is a constant headache. But if the price of seasoned wood continues to spiral, why not use unseasoned? It is about a quarter of the price and can often be obtained for nothing.

There are, of course, problems when using green wood in conventional ways. One solution is to part turn bowls then set them aside for weeks or months to be finish turned later. But apart from the time involved, you need adequate storage space.

Polyethylene glycol (PEG) can be used to season wood, but it is a slow, messy process and the finishes that can be used are limited.

So is there any alternative? The answer, thanks to modern technology, is 'Yes'.

I first became aware of microwave seasoning two or three years ago, after reading an article from New Zealand. Because of the cost and limited availability of seasoned wood and the greater ease of turning unseasoned, not to mention the fascination of trying something different, I decided to experiment.

These experiments have been so successful that I now rarely work in seasoned wood and specialise in green-turned, microwave-seasoned bowls.

My only problem now is size – I will soon have to look beyond the standard microwave to one which can take the bigger bowls I hope to make. But that, as they say, is another story.

Before going on to microwave seasoning, it might be helpful if I give a few details about woods I use and how I turn bowls suitable for the process.

I have not yet found an unsuitable wood for microwave seasoning, although those with a high resin content could behave dangerously in the oven. Ash, cherry, chestnut, laburnum and holly all behave well, but more care has to be taken with yew and beech,

which tend to split.

I use logs which have either been sawn in half or split down the middle. But however you get there, the basic raw material is a half log as long as it is broad.

I usually mount a log of up to about 255mm (10in) diameter on a screw chuck and anything larger on a faceplate ring. One disadvantage of using unseasoned wood is it is heavier per cubic foot than seasoned.

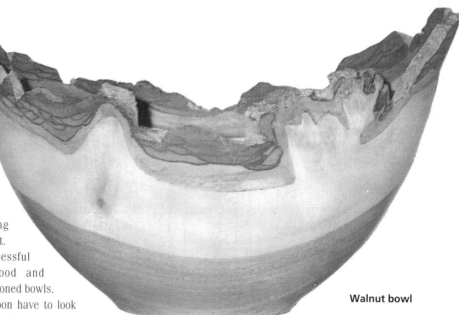

Walnut bowl

Keep it flat

For either mounting, a flat area in the middle of the curved surface of the half log should be cut. My electric chainsaw does this job in less than a minute but, however you do it, the surface cut should be flat and parallel to the flat surface of the half log and big enough to take the chuck.

For those who prefer the pin chuck, this stage will not be

necessary. Personally, I find pin chucks used in green wood have a tendency to work loose.

The size of half log to be turned determines whether I remove corners or cut a round blank with the band saw. On a log of up to about 230mm (9in) diameter, I would not remove anything before mounting on the lathe, but from there to about 280mm (11in) I would cut off the corners and above that cut a round blank, dynamic balance being my main priority.

Having mounted the wood onto a chuck, I then turn the outside of the bowl to shape, not forgetting to include a recess or a spigot on the base to hold the work while turning the inside. I turn a recess oversize, to allow for shrinkage.

I use a Craft Supplies Precision Combination Chuck and for small or purely decorative bowls tend to use the spigot attachment. For bigger bowls and those more functional, I use the expanding collets, which are more secure.

Before removing the half-turned bowl from the screw or faceplate chuck, I sand the outside, if the wood is not too wet. If it is, the abrasive paper or cloth will clog almost instantly, making it impossible to continue.

Sanding before seasoning, if possible, makes life easier, but great care must be taken, and if you use a hand-held abrasive I advise you to sand with the lathe still.

You are dealing with an irregular surface and fingers can easily be damaged if you do this job with the lathe turning. I use a powered Velcro system, but even here you must be careful.

The half-turned bowl should now be reversed for mounting on spigot or expanding collet jaws, and the inside turned to finished dimensions. Extreme care must be taken again, and turning the inside should not be attempted by beginners or the inexperienced.

The gouge will not be cutting into a flat surface where it would be in contact with the work at all times. Particularly when you get to the last cuts, where you begin the cut at the outside edge, your gouge will only be in contact with the work or a small percentage of each revolution of the lathe. The rest of the time it will be unsupported in thin air.

Half log – the starting point

The round blank cut from the half log with faceplate ring fitted

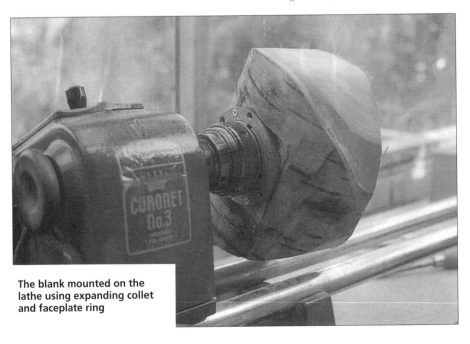

The blank mounted on the lathe using expanding collet and faceplate ring

Turning at speed, the high points on a natural edge bowl are nearly invisible, and therefore dangerous. For this same reason, more experienced woodturners should be reminded that you cannot support the outside of the bowl with your free hand while making finishing cuts to the inside, as you would with a regularly shaped bowl. Finishing cuts should only be done with very sharp tools.

I would offer the same advice for sanding the inside of the bowl as sanding the outside, but add that even more care is needed. No hand-sanding should be attempted while the lathe is in motion. Remember, fingers are more precious than time.

At this stage, examine the bark to see if it is attached securely. If it is then it's a bonus; if not, it should be removed.

For microwave seasoning, as uniform a cross-section as possible should be aimed for, although the base will usually be a little thicker.

Work quickly

It is also important when turning green wood to work quickly. This is more necessary with some woods than others, yew and beech, as I mentioned earlier, being particularly susceptible to cracking and splitting.

If I have to break off at any time while turning a bowl, I cover it with a damp

The outside turning has now been completed, including the recess to take the expanding collet.

The part-turned bowl reversed on the lathe

The setting of the oven timer depends on the size of the bowl – one minute for bowls up to about 200mm (8in), two minutes for those between 200mm (8in) and 305mm (12in), and three minutes for bowls over 305mm (12in).

I then start the oven and, at the end of the cycle, remove the bowl and allow it to cool. Bowls can vary from being slightly warm to quite hot when they leave the oven. The cooling time will depend upon size, thickness and moisture content, but I suggest you leave them for at least half an hour.

Once cooled, the bowl goes back in the oven, but this time upside down and turned at 90° to the first cycle. This isn't necessary if an oven turntable is being used. The operation is then repeated.

For the third cycle I place the bowl in the oven the right way up, but turn it another 90°. Allow the same cooling period. The fourth time, I position the bowl in the oven upside down, turning it 90° again, then removing to cool.

The reason for changing its position in the microwave is because each oven has hotter and cooler spots and the changes ensure the heat is distributed more evenly.

I now reweigh the bowl and record the weight with the original. It should show a slight reduction.

Except for larger sizes, it should now be safe to leave bowls overnight at normal room temperature and atmosphere. However, if I am not able to carry out any more microwave sessions that day on large bowls, then I place them in a cooler atmosphere,

cloth and a polythene bag. Even when the turning is completed, I take the same precaution if I can't start seasoning at once.

I like to get finished bowls into the microwave as soon as they come off the lathe. I use a standard domestic microwave oven with a 700 Watt maximum output, with no turntable, and all my directions are based on this. Not that I think any major adjustments would have to be made using most of the microwave ovens on the market, but I can't accept liability for accidents or problems which may arise as a result. Having said that, I don't see why you should not carry out problem-free seasoning in your microwave.

After turning a bowl, the next thing to do is to weigh it and record the weight. Kitchen scales are adequate for this. I then place the bowl in the middle of the microwave and set to defrost.

usually in a polythene bag. If I don't take this precaution, cracking or splitting of the rim can occur.

When I resume the microwave sessions, I repeat the programme of four cycles, allowing at least an hour between each programme, until the bowl's weight stays the same for two successive programmes. The bowl is now seasoned, but should be set aside for several days in a reasonably dry atmosphere before carrying out finishing operations.

If the bowl was too wet to sand after I had completed the turning, this is my next job, and I therefore re-chuck it on the lathe. It will not revolve as truly as when it came off the lathe after turning, sometimes by a little and sometimes by a lot. I would therefore suggest sanding is carried out with the lathe stationary. A fast-turning, out-of-true, natural-edge bowl is no respecter of

The bowl with the inside fully turned

The gouge position at the high side of the bowl

The gouge position at the low side of the bowl

The bowl after seasoning, re-mounting on the lathe and sanding

fingers or anything else that gets in its way.

One of the advantages of microwave seasoning is that any finish can be applied to the completed bowl. I use a sanding sealer, which is sanded down when dry, followed by a coat of melamine. This I rub down with fine wire wool before applying several coats of wax polish, buffed between coats.

Last job

One last job remains to be done. The bottoms of bowls seasoned in microwaves are not flat. For those turned using the expanding collet jaws I sand the bottoms flat by holding them against a large (at least 200mm (8in)) diameter sanding disc rotating on the lathe. For those that were turned using a spigot chuck, the spigot must be removed in the usual way.

Microwave seasoning has opened up a whole new world of turning for me. I have had disasters along the way, but am pleased to say they now are rare.

Bowls have, on a number of occasions, been accidently exposed to the microwave's full power. They all survived – but I think that was more luck than judgement.

This article originally appeared in *Woodturning* issue 17, November 1993.

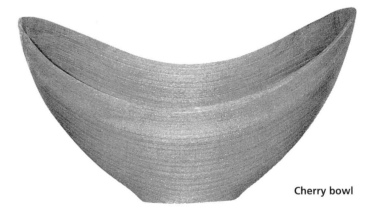

Cherry bowl

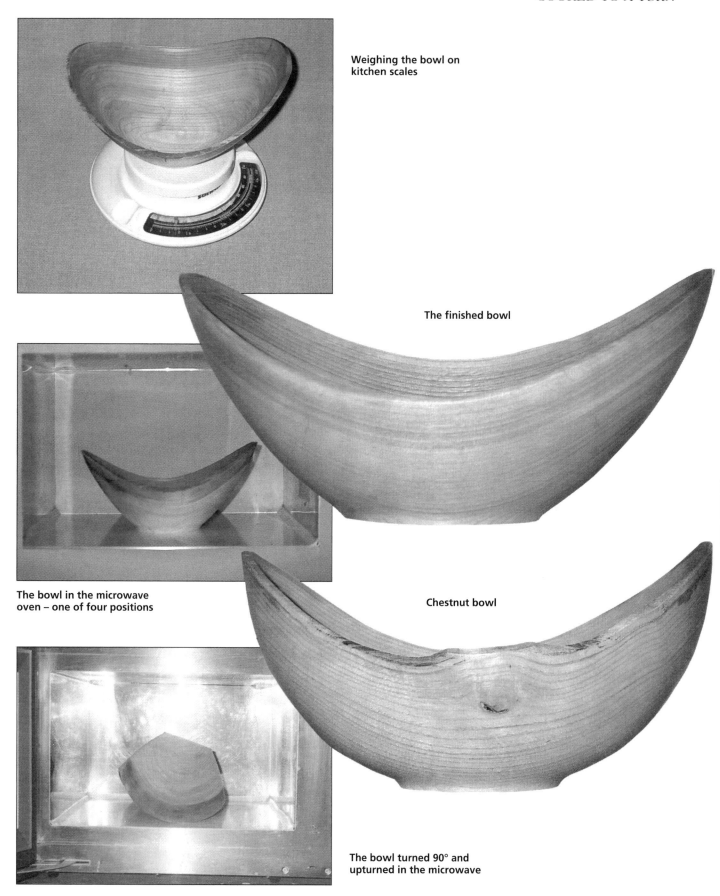

Weighing the bowl on
kitchen scales

The finished bowl

The bowl in the microwave
oven – one of four positions

Chestnut bowl

The bowl turned 90° and
upturned in the microwave

Turning green

What is green woodturning? Do bowls crack when they dry? What are the best finishes to use? These are just some of the questions which Viv and Shirley Collins answer here.

Viv & Shirley Collins

Green woodturning is fun, cheap and challenging. Most of the available modern lathes can be used, so long as the greater weight of a green wood blank, as opposed to a dry wood blank, is taken into consideration.

Rather than concentrate on the individual aspects, it is best viewed as a complete process from log to finished bowl. Most of the problems experienced with green woodturning occur because one or other aspect has been neglected.

Gardens, parks, sawmills and so on, all yield a rich harvest for the turner of wet wood. Green wood is easily obtained from local sawmills or council tree-felling departments. You may be charged a small fee, but usually wood destined for burning is given free. Once friends and neighbours know you are interested in newly-felled logs, you will be inundated with offers and pleas to 'remove the tree we've just cut down in the back garden'.

Woods delightful to turn are ash and sycamore, which send long, fine shavings flying over your shoulder. These bowls are easy to dry.

English oak is my favourite, being a wonderful wood to turn wet. The only drawback is the tannic acid content, which will corrode and turn black any unprotected metal surfaces. Coat all tools and equipment with WD40 or wax as a precautionary measure.

English yew is a surprisingly different experience turned green. Try it and see.

Hawthorn, if a big enough piece can be obtained, produces a beautiful bowl. This wood will change colour with sunflower oil, turning a delicate orange.

Cherry is an excellent wood for thin-walled bowls. But take care when drying, as the sapwood shrinks faster than the heartwood, causing extra distortion.

These are some of the easily-obtained woods you can use, but generally any wood with a specific gravity greater than 0.46 can be reliably turned into a bowl that will not crack. However, not all this bounty is suitable for the lathe. The first thing to be understood is how to choose a suitable log.

A good log in a turner's terms is one free from branches and reasonably cylindrical throughout its length (Photo 1). The trunk of the tree is the obvious first choice, although large branches can also yield good sized blanks.

1. A good log

2. Bowl shapes drawn correctly on to a log

3. Wrong alignment of bowl in end grain

4. Slicing the log in half with a chainsaw

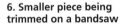

5. Note circle drawn is offset, as the centre of the circle is in the pith

6. Smaller piece being trimmed on a bandsaw

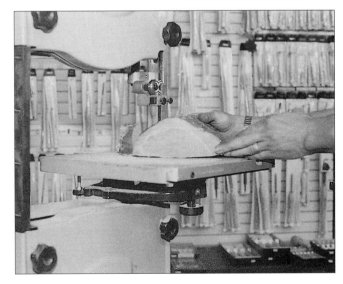

I use an electric chainsaw to cut logs into blanks, but have learnt to treat it with respect. Always ensure the log to be cut is properly supported. The best recommendation is to do a chainsaw safety course. Remember, the aim is to cut bits off the log, not off you.

Photo 2 shows the end of log with two bowl shapes drawn onto it. These have been placed to lie symmetrically across the grain, so the heart of the log runs through the middle of the bowl.

The shape of the growth rings is equal in both halves of each bowl so producing an oval bowl. Photo 3 shows wrong alignment.

Chalk a line through the heart of the log and split it in half, after ensuring it is firmly supported (Photo 4). Holding the chainsaw at a slight angle to the horizontal will produce shorter shavings and prevent clogging the blade. If you do produce long shavings and clog the machine, unplug the chainsaw before clearing the blade.

With the flat side of the log uppermost, place a compass point into the pith or heart of the log. But not in the physical centre. This ensures the heart runs through the middle of the bowl blank (Photo 5). Draw a circle.

To lessen the weight of the blank I trim the corners, making physical handling easier and reducing stress on the lathe bearings. Smaller pieces may be trimmed round on a bandsaw (Photo 6).

Now a decision has to be made which will affect the shape of the finished bowl. Placing the faceplate on the flat surface of the log will result in a bowl where the rim either side of the heart will curve downward (Photo 7). Alternatively, placing the faceplate on a flat circle on the curved or bark side of the log will cause the rim to curve upwards (Photo 8).

As most of my work is on larger bowls, I use a 150mm (6in) faceplate attached with four M10 or M8 coach screws. These are stronger and safer than ordinary woodscrews and one set of four may be used repeatedly. The blank is now ready for mounting (Photo 9).

Mounting small pieces of green wood should not present any problems, but for larger pieces (some of mine weigh up to 3 cwt) another pair of hands is extremely useful for lifting the blank onto the lathe.

We are now ready to turn. Start your machine at the lowest speed. I use a Poolewood PW28-40, which gives a low speed of 250

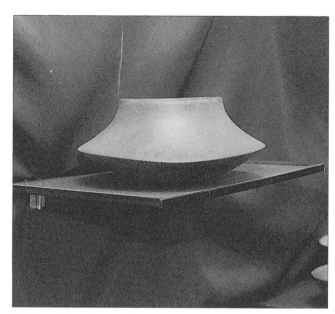

8. Placing faceplate on the bark side causes the rim to curve up either side of the heart

7. Faceplate position on heart side of a log causes the rim to curve downwards

rpm which easily handles a blank 660mm (26in) diameter x 305mm (12in) thick (Photo 10).

When you start the machine, keep your hand near the Off button in case of initial emergencies. When you are happy with the balance of the blank it is time to move onto shaping your bowl.

With an irregular shape the initial roughing cuts should be light as the bark is removed. I use a 20mm (¾in) long-handled Sorby bowl gouge, as it has the weight and balance to do this job with ease (Photo 11).

The overall design of your bowl is personal, but take into account at the initial stages the alteration in shape that will occur with the drying, and use this to complement your work.

While shaping the outside, it is advisable on a large bowl to true up the front face of the blank at the same time.

If possible, do some initial hollowing to help reduce the weight of the blank before reverse chucking.

Everybody has their pet chucks. Mine are the Poolewood Supachuck and the Multistar. Both have expanding and contracting dovetail jaws. Use the Multistar for work up to 510mm (20in) diameter and the Poolewood Supachuck with the wet-turning dovetail jaws fitted for blanks up to 660mm (26in) diameter.

Whether you turn a recess or a spigot on the base of the bowl for the chuck, remember that when the bowl dries the bottom of the bowl will have to be sanded or cross-planed flat (Photo 12).

When sanding green wood, I prefer to use car body wet and dry paper from 180 to 320 grade, lubricated with ordinary tap water. A big advantage is the paper does not clog while sanding. Also, it does not produce dust – an important consideration for your lungs. However, this does not preclude the use of a dust mask and safety goggles.

Hollowing the inside follows the usual procedure, but special note needs to be taken of wall thicknesses. Paper-thin walls are not a necessity – 6mm (¼in) thick walls are perfectly all right, although the drying time will be increased. Choose the wall thickness to suit your design.

Again, using wet and dry paper, sand the inside. Ensure the vessel holding the sanding water is kept well away from the electrical parts of the machine. Do not touch any unprotected switches with wet hands.

When sanding has been completed a dry rag, held securely in the palm of the hand, is moved over the bowl to remove any excess water and to dry the surface before finishing.

10. A 305mm x 180mm (12in x 7in) yew log mounted on a Poolewood PW 28-40 lathe

Finishing

I am often asked at shows how to stop a bowl cracking, but nobody asks why it cracks in the first place. Maybe that is the problem. Rather than concentrating on techniques, the characteristics of the material need to be understood.

The tension set up by the end grain drying before the side grain in the walls causes a bowl to crack. The remedy is to slow down the drying of the end grain to the same rate as that of the side grain.

This is achieved by using an oil finish and a controlled micro-environment. Having experimented with many different oils the following have proved to be the most successful.

Pure sunflower oil is readily available and produces a matt finish. If using this, or indeed any oil, keep it in a special bottle in the workshop. **Never use the same oil bottle for cooking purposes, as the contents could become contaminated.**

Remove your bowl from the lathe and apply two or three thick coats of oil, paying special attention to the end grain as the wood will suck up the oil like a sponge.

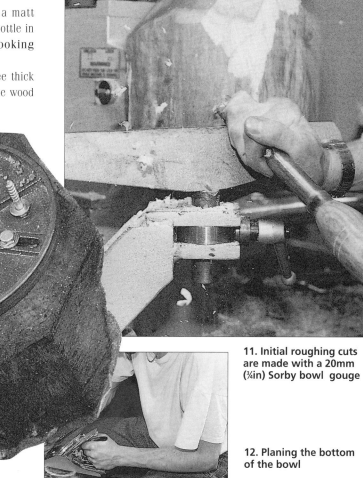

9. Yew log mounted to a 200mm (8in) faceplate with M8 x 40 coach screws

11. Initial roughing cuts are made with a 20mm (¾in) Sorby bowl gouge

12. Planing the bottom of the bowl

Place the bowl in a sealed plastic bag. Over the next six to seven days, open the bag daily and give another heavy coat, paying special attention to end grain and dry patches. Reseal the bag after each application.

Olive oil (first pressing only) is more expensive, but for prized bowls is well worth using. Follow the same procedures as above.

Raw linseed oil is another cheap oil producing a satin finish. Again follow the procedures outlined for sunflower oil.

As none of these oils contain drying agents, time is needed for air drying between coats to prevent a sticky build-up. Danish oil, which produces a reasonably shiny finish, does contain drying agents and is therefore applied in the following way.

With the bowl still on the lathe but with the lathe stopped, apply a fairly heavy coating of Danish oil. Leave for five minutes and apply another coat. After 15 minutes wipe off the excess oil with the lathe running and buff to a shine with a soft cloth.

Remove from the lathe, apply oil to the chucking ring and immediately place into a plastic bag, sealing the opening. Supermarket bags are excellent for this. (Warning: do not allow any writing on a supermarket bag to come into contact with your bowl, as it may transfer itself.)

The sealed bag micro-environment is used to prevent moisture escaping, so allowing the bowl's initial tension to be released and the first movement of the wood to take place.

The second movement of the bowl takes place when the wood falls below saturation level. To achieve this in a controlled way and to prevent cracking, the environment in the sealed bag is gradually changed over eight days.

This is simply done. Poke a hole in the bag after two days with your finger. Increase the size of the hole at two day intervals for eight days until the hole is fist-sized. At the end of this time bowls up to 355mm (14in) diameter can be completely removed from the bag. Bowls over this size should stay in the bag for another seven or eight days, increasing the size of the hole as before.

All drying in the bag should take place in a moderate temperature. Too hot and the bowl in the bag will sweat; too cold and drying will not take place.

English oak bowl, 405mm x 150mm (16in x 6in) with 3mm (⅛in) thick wavy rim

Sycamore bowl of inverted cone shape, 210mm x 145mm (8¼in x 5¾in)

Spalted beech bowl 305mm x 180mm (12in x 7in) with 6mm (¼in) rim

Once removed from the bag, leave the bowl in the same room or workshop for another two weeks. At the end of this period it is moved into a warmer atmosphere to continue drying.

A bowl of 150–255mm (6–10in) diameter will take six weeks to dry. Those of 255–380mm (10–15in) diameter will take eight to 12 weeks. These times are averages, based on a 5mm (³⁄₁₆in) wall thickness. Thicker walls will need a longer drying time, thinner walled bowls less.

With experience you will soon find the best rooms and temperatures in your house for drying. As a general rule, bedrooms are usually about the right temperature and humidity for the early drying stages. Kitchens, being warmer, are good for the intermediate drying, and living rooms for the final stages, as these are usually warmest and driest.

When placing the bowl in the living room, make sure it is furthest from the fire or radiator for the first few days, so it becomes accustomed to the atmosphere. After this, the bowl may be moved nearer the heat source, but not over it. Equally, do not leave bowls in the hot sun on a window sill.

Once the bowl has dried, the bottom wll have distorted, so the last job to do is to finish the base. I do not remount my bowls and turn the bottoms off or put patterns in.

Belt sander

I use a belt sander or linisher on smaller bowls to remove the chucking ring and make the base flat. On larger bowls I crossplane the bottoms flat using an ordinary bench plane, holding the bowl steady on a piece of rag. Remember to re-oil the base with your chosen oil. Bowls finished in this way will be waterproof and safe for food usage.

As you can see, this is a fairly simple method of green woodturning that is easy and cheap. It does not involve large outgoings or involved processes. If followed carefully and patiently you should produce successful green bowls, but be prepared for the occasional rogue wood.

Normal safety procedures should be employed at all times. Have fun and remember – the wetter the better.

This article originally appeared in *Woodturning* issue 19, February 1994.

A fine Finnish

Laminating wood has been popular in Scandinavia for decades. Here a self-taught woodturner from Finland describes his work and methods.

Matti Laurila

I have always liked using laminated woods. My first work on the lathe was with plywood, making candlesticks, plates and bowls.

Once I was able to get a cheap batch of 3mm (⅛in) oak and birch veneers which I laminated to make bowls of different colours inside and out.

I use some home-grown woods such as birch (including veneers and plywood), masur birch, juniper and apple. Recently I have mostly used imported woods like teak, African and American walnut, Honduran mahogany, wenge, Santos rosewood, Oregon pine, oak, beech and ash.

Usually the imported wood is dry, but five or six types I have got from England have developed splits. Another problem I have is with Finnish curled birch, which has to dry for at least a year. It is easy to turn, but there are sometimes dry black knots inside, hidden by a perfect exterior.

My workshop is a garage of 20 square metres. I have two lathes, a Swedish Ejca and a table model, a circular saw and band saw, mortiser, cramp frame and lots of hand tools.

Lately I have concentrated on making platters by laminating several different types of wood in layers. This involves a lot of cutting, planing and gluing, and some turning. Most of the platters are one-offs and can take a whole week to make. I also make platters from solid wood, sometimes with a border of a contrasting colour, and candlesticks which are easier and can be made in

**Laminated candlesticks in
various woods 100mm (4in) –
170mm (6¾in) high**

**Oak and birch veneer bowl
160mm (6¼in) high x
280mm (11in) diameter**

Curled birch mugs ('kuksas' in Lapland), 85mm (3¼in) high. The figures, copied from ancient rock paintings, were carved and filled with glue and pigment.

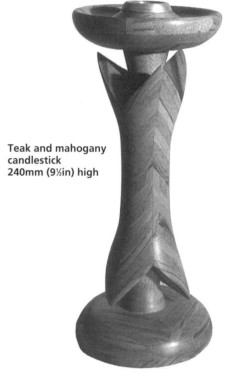

Teak and mahogany candlestick 240mm (9½in) high

batches.

Perhaps my favourite wood is wenge, which is really beautiful but very hard and dusty to work – I have to take a sauna in the evening! To work it I use a Luna Speedcut tool in which I can use different blades. I have made about 30 blades from old planer knives of various shapes and widths so I do not have to keep going to the sharpening stone.

I also have a Luna Speedy cutting tool. This uses small HSS blades which are hard to sharpen and expensive when ordered from Sweden. I have made two handles, one round and the other rhomboid, or diamond-shaped, to hold cheaper HSS blades.

1

2

3

4

5

6

7

8

For laminating the wood I use white wood glue. For finishing I use Rustins Danish oil on darker woods, and a Finnish natural lacquer on lighter woods, applied by brush. I apply four coats, sanding between each. For the final coat I use a two-part mix including a catalyst.

Here is how I make a platter with a decorative patterned centre. As I am a simple amateur, my methods may appear primitive and complicated to professionals!

First I glue together three lengths of 10mm x 45mm (⅜in x 1¾in) teak and mahogany into bars. Half are teak-mahogany-teak, and half mahogany-teak-mahogany. I saw these into equal sections with the saw set at 45° (Photo 1). Then I glue and cramp the sections together into cubes with a square section in the centre (Photo 2). The cubes are glued and cramped into strips of five and then into blocks of 30 (Photo 3). These blocks are turned to shape using templates for both internal and external curves (Photo 4),

I laminate the outer part or rim of the platter from the same woods. I cut three discs and cut out circles from the centre of them to take the decorative centre (Photo 5). After gluing, the discs are

Oak and birch
veneer bowl,
195mm (7¾in) high
x 260mm (10¼in) diameter

9

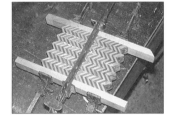

10

11

12

turned to shape to take the insert (Photo 6). Then the insert is glued in place (Photo 7). Photo 8 shows me with the finished platter in my workshop.

Other laminations can be made up to form different patterns. In Photo 9 strips of different woods 10mm x 50mm (⅜in x 2in) have been

Laminated platters in various woods, 280mm – 420mm (11in – 16½in) diameter

laminated together and are sawn into strips at 45° (Photo 10). These are then further laminated into chevron patterns (Photo 11). Lots of different patterns can be made up in this way (Photo 12).

Luna tools are stocked by Essve (UK) Ltd.

This article originally appeared in *Woodturning* issue 14, May/June 1993.

The Authors

A short biography about each of the
contributing authors in this book

Dick Bew

Dick Bew lives in the West Country,
having retired from his second career as
Brixham Harbour Master. His main
career was as a Seaman Officer in the
Royal Navy for 35 years, during which
time he travelled worldwide. The 'turning
bug' bit him in New Zealand when on loan
service to the Royal New Zealand Navy in
the 1960s. Since then he has pursued
woodturning where possible when shore-
based.

Since retiring, his main activity has
been to develop various aspects of
segmented and spiral segmented turning.
The main concern was to save wood. The
luxury of turning an exotic wooden bowl
with 90% ending up as shavings was no
longer viable. The off-cuts from segmented
work were then used to produce stickwork
for inlay, adding another dimension to
segmented turning.

Dick Bew has exhibited his stickware
and segmented turning at various shows
and local craft fairs, and is a member of
the AWGB belonging to the Devon Branch.

Albert Clarke

Albert Clarke has been a lifelong
woodworker. He worked for 27 years as a
wood model maker with NACA (now
NASA), the American National Aeronautics
and Space Administration.

He made prototype patterns for aircraft
and encountered many interesting
challenges, some requiring special jigs
and fixtures.

During the early 1940s he worked at
The Ames Research Center in California,
where he helped develop the famous P51
Mustang fighter aircraft.

He made accurate carved wind tunnel
models from metal and Honduran
mahogany. He and most of his colleagues
were members of the pattern-makers
union.

Now in his seventies, he is retired, but
still enjoying woodturning at his home in
Marshall, California. He turns for fun, but
also sells his work.

Albert's work was featured in the
International Lathe Turned Objects Show
in Philadelphia in 1991.

Viv and Shirley Collins

Undaunted by the recession, Viv and
Shirley Collins launched Simply Wood,
their Oxford-based woodturning business,
in 1992. Viv abandoned a career in
electronics and Shirley hers in special
needs teaching.

Viv, an innovator, was attracted to
experimenting with large lumps of green
wood and together they developed a
successful process for green-turned
bowls.

Their first major show was with
Poolewood Equipment in Nottingham,
where Viv's green turning demonstrations
were enthusiastically received.

This was soon followed by further
woodworking shows at Bristol,
Manchester, Sandown and the NEC at
Birmingham.

They have now joined forces with
Poolewood to set up a Woodturning School
and Supplies Centre. Details of their
turning and green wood courses can be
obtained from: Unit W2, Lenton Business
Centre, Lenton Boulevard, Nottingham
NG7 2BY.

Ernie Conover

Ernie Conover teaches woodworking in
general, and woodturning in particular, at
Conover Workshops, Ohio, a school he and
his wife Susan operate together. In
addition to writing and lecturing widely,
he is a technical consultant to a number of
companies on design and manufacture of
woodworking tools and machines.

Mike Foden

Mike Foden, born in Southport,
Merseyside, has been woodturning for
about 10 years. He did not start turning
until in his early forties, and is entirely
self-taught. About seven years ago he
acquired a metal-working lathe and
enrolled on a model engineering course at
night school. He gave it up after three
weeks as there was only one tutor for 20
students, all needing personal tuition.
However, after much trial and error, he is
now a competent metal machinist, once
again entirely self-taught.

As Mike has a full time office job, he
turns purely as a hobby at weekends and
in the evenings. Even so, his work has
been accepted by many leading galleries
in this country, and some of his pieces
have been sent abroad. He specializes in
ornamental turning and most of his work
is in African blackwood which is extremely
hard and, he feels, the only really suitable
timber for OT. His lathes have been a
Coronet Elf, a Coronet No 3 and latterly a
Myford ML10.

Mike readily admits that he is never
fully satisfied with his work and is
continually striving for improvements, an
outlook which he also applies to his
turning equipment.

Geoff Heath

Geoff Heath is a self-taught amateur
turner who has been slowly improving his
skills over the past 17 years. Starting
with a very small Arundel lathe and a

boxed set of three basic tools he moved on to a Tyme Cub, and now owns a Coronet No 3.

He undertakes small commissions, and also sells his work through three local shops and at two craft fairs a year. In 1988 he retired from his employment as Chief Structural Engineer of the Manchester unit of British Aerospace and so has plenty of time to indulge his hobby.

He enjoys solving problems, especially ones which involve some mathematics, and has also been known to devise mathematical puzzles.

Geoff's approach to turning is conditioned by his working life as an engineer concerned with the structural integrity of new aircraft designs. In the aircraft industry, design, backed by research and proved by analysis and test, precedes any production, and Geoff finds it natural to adopt this approach to turning.

Besides being a member of the AWGB, Geoff is a Chartered Engineer, a Fellow of the Institution of Mechanical Engineers and a Fellow of the Royal Aeronautical Society.

W T Hughes

Bill Hughes took up woodturning as an evening relaxation from daytime commercial office pressures. Five years after retiring it is his main relaxation. He is one of the founder members of the West Sussex Woodturners.

Kurt Johansson

Born just south of the Arctic Circle in 1940, in the little Swedish Lapland town of Moskosel, Kurt Johansson was an apprentice cabinetmaker for four years, then journeyman cabinetmaker. He further extended his skills by studying blacksmithing, toolmaking and other aspects of engineering, culminating in his training as a teacher. Since 1964 he has taught Swedish *Slöjd*, as fortunately Sweden still ensures that craft skills are included in the school curriculum.

Kurt divides his time between teaching, turning for galleries and commissioned pieces, and preparing for exhibitions. He

is in great demand in Sweden and elsewhere as a demonstrator and is widely regarded as a natural teacher. He enjoys experimenting with new tools and turning equipment and is a consultant to Swedish lathe and tool manufacturers.

Apart from his own experimentation with form and design, Kurt, who now lives at Marieholm in southern Sweden, maintains the best in traditional Swedish turning. When he occasionally decorates pieces, these follow restrained regional patterns from the area where Johansson was born. This part of Lapland is the most rewarding for those visiting Sweden who wish to see the best of *Same* (Lappish crafts).

Matti Laurila

Matti Laurila is in his early sixties, and has lived all his life in Jarvenpaa, a small town near Finland's capital city of Helsinki. He started woodwork at the age of 10 and it has been his hobby for over 20 years.

He began turning in 1980 on a drill-powered lathe, and is entirely self-taught. Since retiring four years ago, after 30 years as supervisor of a cooperative wholesale business, woodwork has been his full-time occupation and he enjoys inventing and experimenting with new ideas and techniques.

Matti began making furniture in the 1950s when he got married and couldn't afford to buy any. He had only a saw, hammer, plane and chisel and little skill or experience, but plenty of enthusiasm and energy.

Since then he has replaced the furniture many times, with better design and craftsmanship each time.

His turned work is sometimes exhibited in business offices and shop windows.

Terry Martin

Terry Martin was born in Melbourne in 1947. A graduate of Armidale College, Adelaide, and the University of New England, New South Wales, he has had a satisfying and adventurous life travelling the world in various capacities, including Stage Manager of the Royal Opera House,

Covent Garden, Ski Patrol in Austria, geological exploration in the Pacific Islands and Migrant Education in Australia.

A growing appreciation of fine craft work was heightened by several years spent in Japan, and when Terry returned to Australia he decided to pursue his interest in woodcraft.

Terry believes that woodturning allows use of limited timber resources for maximum effect. Much of the wood he uses is recycled, such as fence posts or railway sleepers. Influenced by Japanese ceramics and other crafts, he believes that the natural faults of the timber should be allowed to remain to enhance the work he does on the wood.

Ann and Bob Phillips

Ann Phillips graduated from Massey University with a first class honours degree in science and continued her research work overseas, gaining her doctorate in the UK.

Bob served in the RAF and later worked in the charter airline industry as an aeronautical engineer.

Back in New Zealand Ann took up a post with the agricultural research division in Upper Hutt while Bob worked first as an engineer and then as a weights and measures inspector.

After six years pursuing successful careers the couple, still in their early thirties, decided on a career change. They threw in their jobs to have a go at being self-employed and running their own business.

The couple became full-time professional woodturners eight years ago and have never looked back. They now supply shops and galleries throughout New Zealand and some of their pieces are held in overseas collections.

Dave Regester

Dave Regester has been turning professionally since 1974. In his workshop at Tiverton in Devon he makes salad bowls, scoops and platters, which he sells through high-quality kitchenware shops.

He also makes one-off artistic pieces which he sells through galleries and exhibitions.

Helen Sanderson

Helen Sanderson took up woodturning seriously only about three years ago, having taken early retirement from higher education.

Although largely self-taught, Helen decided some professional help might speed up the learning process and took a couple of weekend courses – one with Reg Sherwin and the other with Ray Key. She owes them, she acknowledges, a considerable debt. Ray was probably responsible for her interest in bowls.

Finding seasoned wood so expensive, and having read an article on microwave seasoning, Helen decided to experiment. She has spent the past two years concentrating almost solely on developing the process of microwave seasoning natural edge bowls.

At present, Helen sells her work through major craft fairs, but she hopes in the near future to expand into the craft shop and gallery end of the market.

Her work has been shown at a number of exhibitions. At the 1991 Loughborough Seminar, one of her bowls was among the 40 pieces selected to represent the Association of Woodturners of Great Britain.

She lives at Ratcliffe Culey, Atherstone, Warwickshire.

Merryll Saylan

Merryll Saylan started her turning in 1974. Having graduated from UCLA in 1973 she enrolled in the woodworking programme and turning was a requirement. Turn something, she was told. She had been doing Chinese cooking so she turned out a rice bowl – in fact six of them.

Her art school background has much to do with her feeling for colours and textures. Her approach to turning is similarly distinctive. She measures her wood and draws the shape she wants before she starts working. She says timber is rare and she doesn't want to waste it. 'If I draw a shape which is really beautiful, when I start turning I keep going until I have reached that shape'.

Merryll is well known in the UK as a result of her twelve month residency at the Grizedale Forestry Centre in the Lake District and the demonstrations she gave in 1991–2 at the International Practical Woodturning Exhibition at Wembley, and also at the Loughborough '91 International Seminar.

Johannes Volmer

Johannes Volmer grew up in Dresden, the kings' residence of Saxonia, famous for its baroque architecture, art galleries, china and museums.

Following the town's destruction at the end of the war, he was forced, as a pupil and student, to work in several shops. He gained experience of many kinds of handicraft, and the machining of woods and metals, which led to his becoming a machine designer at Chemnitz, an industrial centre of machinery.

Johannes graduated from the Technical University of Dresden, and has taught mechanics and design of mechanisms for over 30 years as a full professor at the Technical University of Chemnitz.

Germany's oldest woodworking region – the nearby Ore Mountains (Erzebirge) – has ancient traditions and unique turning techniques still in use today. Woodturning is widely practised there. These circumstances persuaded Johannes, some 18 years ago, to devote himself to the theory and practice of the almost forgotten art of oval turning. His studies resulted in his designing novel oval mechanisms which he tested himself.

He is convinced that once turners have been introduced to oval turning, they will be keen to add it to their repertoire.

Bibliography

DESCH, H.E. *Timber: Its Structure, Properties and Utilization*, 6th edition revised by J M Dinwoodie, Macmillan Press

EVANS, J.H. *Ornamental Turnery*, reprinted 1993, Astragel Press, New Jersey

HOADLEY, R. Bruce. *Understanding Wood: A Craftsman's Guide to Wood Technology*, Taunton Press, USA, 1985

HOLTZAPFFEL, John Jacob. *Turning and Mechanical Manipulation on the Lathe*, 5 volumes, Holtzapffel & Co., London 1846

Volume 1, Materials: Their Differences, Choice, Preparation (out of print)

Volume 2, The Principles of Construction (out of print)

Volume 3, Abrasive and Miscellaneous Processes (out of print)

Volume 4, Hand or Simple Turning, Dover Publications, 1976

Volume 5, Ornamental or Complex Turning, Dover Publications, 1976

KNOX, Frank M. *Ornamental Turnery: A Practical and Historical Approach to a Centuries Old Craft*, Prentice Hall, New York, 1986

NICHOLSON, Peter. *Mechanical Exercises*, London, 1812 (out of print)

PINTO, Edward H. *Treen and Other Wooden Bygones: An Encyclopaedia and Social History*, Bell & Hyman, London, 1969

RAFFAN, Richard. *Turned-Bowl Design*, The Taunton Press, Connecticut, 1987

REGESTER, David. *Woodturning: Step by Step*, B T Batsford, 1993

ROWLEY, Keith. *Woodturning: A Foundation Course*, GMC Publications, 1990

SAINSBURY, John. *Guide to Woodturning Tools and Equipment*, David & Charles, 1989

Metric conversion table

Inches to Millimetres and Centimetres

MM – millimetres   CM – Centimetres

Inches	MM	CM	Inches	CM	Inches	CM
⅛	3	0.3	9	22.9	30	76.2
¼	6	0.6	10	25.4	31	78.7
⅜	10	1.0	11	27.9	32	81.3
½	13	1.3	12	30.5	33	83.8
⅝	16	1.6	13	33.0	34	86.4
¾	19	1.9	14	35.6	35	88.9
⅞	22	2.2	15	38.1	36	91.4
1	25	2.5	16	40.6	37	94.0
1¼	32	3.2	17	43.2	38	96.5
1½	38	3.8	18	45.7	39	99.1
1¾	44	4.4	19	48.3	40	101.6
2	51	5.1	20	50.8	41	104.1
2½	64	6.4	21	53.3	42	106.7
3	76	7.6	22	55.9	43	109.2
3½	89	8.9	23	58.4	44	111.8
4	102	10.2	24	61.0	45	114.3
4½	114	11.4	25	63.5	46	116.8
5	127	12.7	26	66.0	47	119.4
6	152	15.2	27	68.6	48	121.9
7	178	17.8	28	71.1	49	124.5
8	203	20.3	29	73.7	50	127.0

Index

A

African blackwood, suitability for ornamental turning 32
air drying 79, 83–4
aliphatic resin glue, used in stickwork 16
angle grinders, using 34–6
anti-skid grooves 50
ash
    suitability for green turning 96
    suitability for microwave drying 91

B

beech, problems with microwave drying 91–2
bench grinders, using 69–71
bleaching, techniques of 37–40
bowls
    avoiding cracks in 99
    etching by sandblasting 61–4
    green turning 84–5, 91–100
    oval 7–11
    'widgets' and 'wheezes' for turning 49–51
boxes
    decorating with stickwork 14–21
    ornamented 30–2
    tips on turning 50–1
boxwood, suitability for ornamental turning 32

C

cabinet drying 79
callipers, using 46, 76
candlesticks, laminated, making 101–2
captive rings, tips on making 47–8
case-hardening, a seasoning defect 79
cedar, suitability for sandblasting 64
centres, turning between, tips on 45
cherry
    suitability for green turning 96
    suitability for microwave drying 91
chestnut, suitability for microwave drying 91
chisels, sharpening 71–2
chroma, defined 42
chucks
    cement 5
    double-sided tape 59
    for oval turning 8–10
    jammed, remedying 57
    paper joint 59–60
    pin 91–2
coasters, decorating with stickwork 14–21

colouring, techniques of 41–4
colour theory, briefly explained 42
conservation, issues of 4–5
copy attachments 75
copy turning, tips on 75–7
Corozo nuts as a material 3–6
cotton-reel holders, disguising screw-holes in 48–9
cranked tools, grinding to shape 74
cyanoacrylate glue
    problems with colouring 43
    used in chucking 5
    used in stickwork 16

D

Danish oil, used as finish 100, 103
deep yellow wood, suitability for thread cutting 27
dehumidifiers 80, 83–4
depth-gauges, using 50
discolourations in wood, removing 39
dividers, used in copy turning 76
Dremel tool, using 30–2, 34–6
duplication, tips on 75–7
duplicators 75
dyes, types of 42

E

ebonising, techniques of 37–40
ebony, suitability for lenticular turning 25
egg cups, making 67, 88
eggs, making 46
end splits, a seasoning defect 79
epoxy resin glue
    colouring 43
    used in stickwork 16
equilibrium moisture content (EMG), defined 81
etching surfaces by sandblasting, techniques of 61–4

F

faceplates, dummy, using 49
finials, making 5
finishes
    for microwave seasoning 94
    for sandblasted work 62
    for water stains 40
Finnish curled birch, problems with splitting 101

fir
    finishing 62
    suitability for sandblasting 64
foam pads and brushes 38
fungal growth, a seasoning problem 80

G

German gouges, using 87–9
goblets
    captive rings on 47
    making 67
Goniostat jig 31–2
gouges, sharpening 72–4
green timber
    advantages of 78
    hoop turning 86–90
    sanding 98
    turning bowls from 84–5, 91–100
grey steel compound, a polish for Tagua 5
grinders
    angle, using 34–6
    rotary, using 34–6

H

hawthorn, green turning 96
heat pump driers 83–4
hide glue
    used in glue and paper joints 58–60
    used in stickwork 16
holly
    suitability for lenticular turning 25
    suitability for microwave drying 91
hook tools, using 65–8, 87, 89
hoop turning, techniques of 86–90
hue, defined 42

I

index head, needed for ornamental turning 13
ivory, suitability for ornamental turning 32

J

jeweller's rouge, a poor polish for Tagua 5
jigs
    for lenticular turning 22–6
    for pencil-holders 51
    for stools 51–3
    see also Goniostat jig

Notes

Notes

Notes

Notes

Titles available from GMC Publications Ltd

Books

Woodworking Plans and Projects	GMC Publications	Making Dolls' House Furniture	Patricia King
40 More Woodworking Plans and Projects	GMC Publications	Making and Modifying Woodworking Tools	Jim Kingshott
Woodworking Crafts Annual	GMC Publications	The Workshop	Jim Kingshott
Woodworkers' Career and Educational Source Book	GMC Publications	Sharpening: The Complete Guide	Jim Kingshott
Woodworkers' Courses & Source Book	GMC Publications	Turning Wooden Toys	Terry Lawrence
Woodturning Techniques:		Making Board, Peg and Dice Games	Jeff & Jennie Loader
The Very Best from *Woodturning* Magazine	GMC Publications	The Complete Dolls' House Book	Jean Nisbett
Green Woodwork	Mike Abbott	The Secrets of the Dolls' House Makers	Jean Nisbett
Making Little Boxes from Wood	John Bennett	Furniture Projects for the Home	Ernest Parrott
Furniture Restoration and Repair for Beginners	Kevin Jan Bonner	Making Money from Woodturning	Ann & Bob Phillips
The Incredible Router	Jeremy Broun	Members' Guide to Marketing	Jack Pigden
Electric Woodwork	Jeremy Broun	Woodcarving Tools and Equipment	Chris Pye
Woodcarving: A Complete Course	Ron Butterfield	Making Tudor Dolls' Houses	Derek Rowbottom
Making Fine Furniture: Projects	Tom Darby	Making Georgian Dolls' Houses	Derek Rowbottom
Restoring Rocking Horses	Clive Green & Anthony Dew	Making Period Dolls' House Furniture	Derek & Sheila Rowbottom
Heraldic Miniature Knights	Peter Greenhill	Woodturning: A Foundation Course	Keith Rowley
Practical Crafts: Seat Weaving	Ricky Holdstock	Turning Miniatures in Wood	John Sainsbury
Multi-centre Woodturning	Ray Hopper	Pleasure and Profit from Woodturning	Reg Sherwin
Complete Woodfinishing	Ian Hosker	Making Unusual Miniatures	Graham Spalding
Woodturning: A Source Book of Shapes	John Hunnex	Adventures in Woodturning	David Springett
Making Shaker Furniture	Barry Jackson	Woodturning Wizardry	David Springett
Upholstery: A Complete Course	David James	Furniture Projects	Rod Wales
Upholstery Techniques and Projects	David James	Decorative Woodcarving	Jeremy Williams
Designing and Making Wooden Toys	Terry Kelly		

Videos

Dennis White Teaches Woodturning	Jim Kingshott	Sharpening the Professional Way
Part 1 Turning Between Centres	Jim Kingshott	Sharpening Turning and Carving Tools
Part 2 Turning Bowls	Ray Gonzalez	Carving a Figure: The Female Form
Part 3 Boxes, Goblets and Screw Threads	David James	The Traditional Upholstery Workshop, Part 1: Stuffover Upholstery
Part 4 Novelties and Projects		
Part 5 Classic Profiles	David James	The Traditional Upholstery Workshop, Part 2: Drop-in and Pinstuffed Seats
Part 6 Twists and Advanced Turning		

Magazines

WOODCARVING   WOODTURNING   BUSINESSMATTERS

GMC Publications regularly produces new books and videos
on a wide range of woodworking and craft subjects,
and an increasing number of specialist magazines,
all available on subscription.
All these publications are available through bookshops and newsagents,
or may be ordered by post from the publishers at
166 High Street, Lewes, East Sussex BN7 1XU,
Telephone (0273) 477374,   Fax (0273) 478606.
Credit card orders are accepted.
Please write or phone for the latest information.